TAKE
NOTE!

TO ACCOMPANY

Geography: Realms
Regions
and Concepts
2000

NINTH EDITION

H. J. de Blij
Marshall University

Peter O. Muller
University of Miami

JOHN WILEY & SONS, INC.
New York • Chichester • Weinheim
Brisbane • Singapore • Toronto

To order books or for customer service call 1-800-CALL-WILEY (225-5945).

ISBN 0-471-35742-1

Printed in the United States of America

10 9 8 7 6 5 4 3 2

Printed and bound by Courier Westford, Inc.

HOW TO USE TAKE NOTE

This easy-to-carry paperback contains many of the illustrations found in your text. When your instructor discusses one of these figures in class, you can annotate the illustration right in this book. This frees you up to concentrate on the lecture rather than having to quickly recreate an illustration in order to annotate it. It also makes it easy to organize your notes for study later on.

The illustrations you'll find in these pages are exact replicas of the illustrations in your textbook. Some images may be slightly fuzzy or may not reflect the true colors of the originals. We chose not to duplicate the quality and color in the textbook so that we could minimize the cost to you. When you use this reasonably-priced notebook alongside your textbook, you've got a powerful organizational and study tool!

CONTENTS

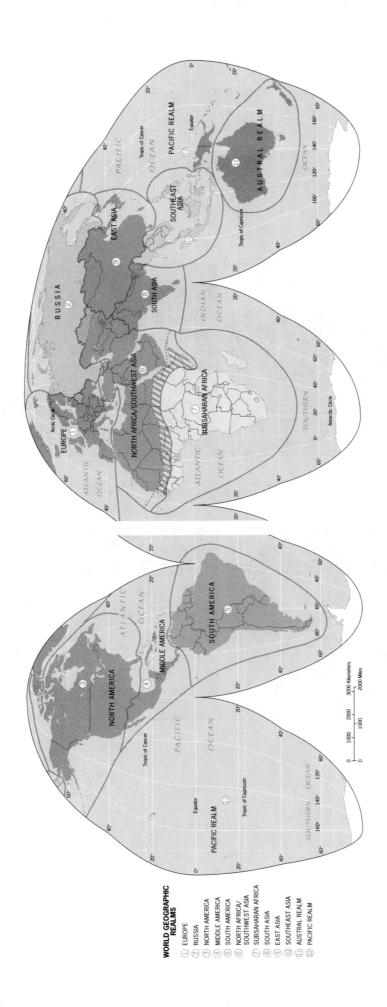

WORLD GEOGRAPHIC REALMS

1. EUROPE
2. RUSSIA
3. NORTH AMERICA
4. MIDDLE AMERICA
5. SOUTH AMERICA
6. NORTH AFRICA/SOUTHWEST ASIA
7. SUBSAHARAN AFRICA
8. SOUTH ASIA
9. EAST ASIA
10. SOUTHEAST ASIA
11. AUSTRAL REALM
12. PACIFIC REALM

FIGURE I-2

EFFECT OF SCALE

0 500 1000 1500 2000 2500 Kilometers

0   500   1000   1500 Miles

1:103,000,000

0   250 500 750 1000 1250 1500 Kilometers

0   250   500   750 Miles

1:53,200,000

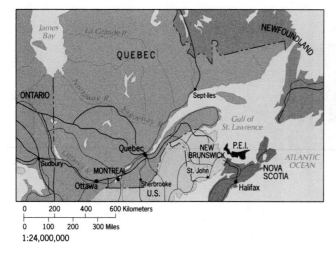

0   200   400   600 Kilometers

0   100   200   300 Miles

1:24,000,000

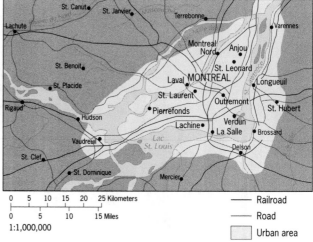

0   5   10   15   20   25 Kilometers

0   5   10   15 Miles

1:1,000,000

—— Railroad
—— Road
☐ Urban area

2

FIGURE I-3

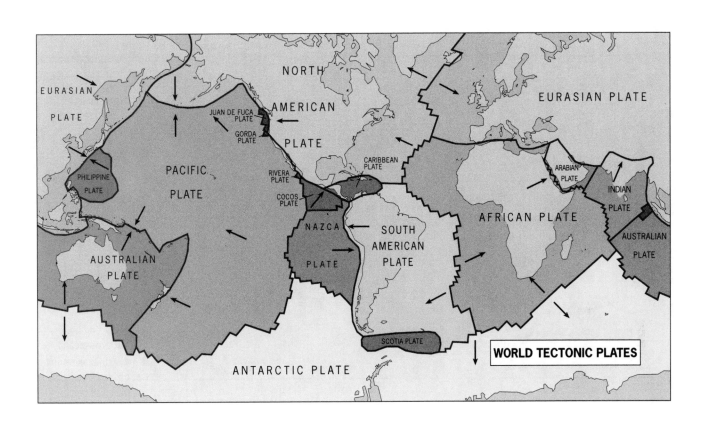

WORLD TECTONIC PLATES

FIGURE I-4

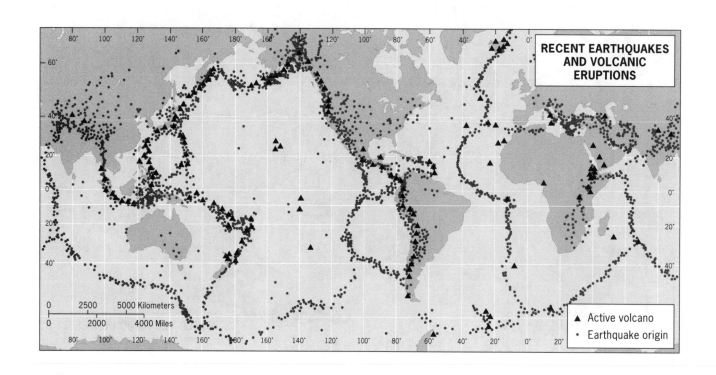

RECENT EARTHQUAKES
AND VOLCANIC
ERUPTIONS

▲ Active volcano
• Earthquake origin

4

FIGURE I-5

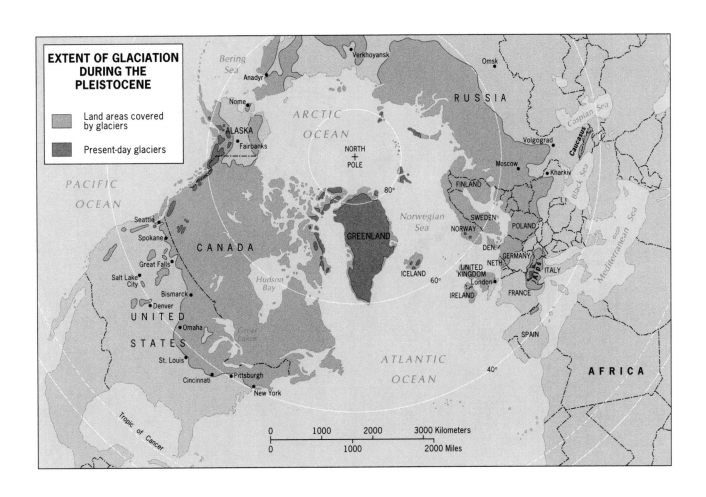

EXTENT OF GLACIATION DURING THE PLEISTOCENE

Land areas covered by glaciers

Present-day glaciers

FIGURE I-6

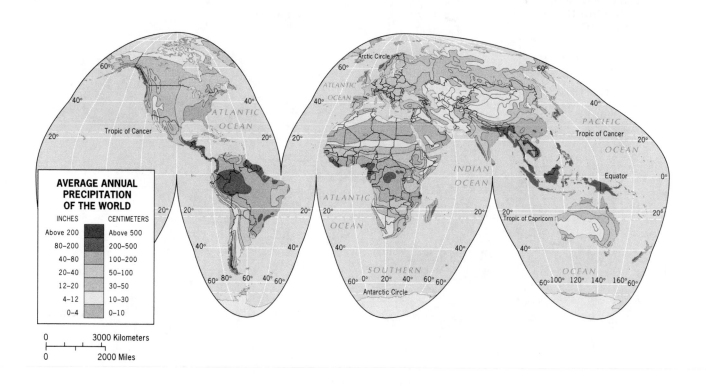

**AVERAGE ANNUAL
PRECIPITATION
OF THE WORLD**

INCHES		CENTIMETERS
Above 200		Above 500
80–200		200–500
40–80		100–200
20–40		50–100
12–20		30–50
4–12		10–30
0–4		0–10

0   3000 Kilometers

0   2000 Miles

6

FIGURE I-7

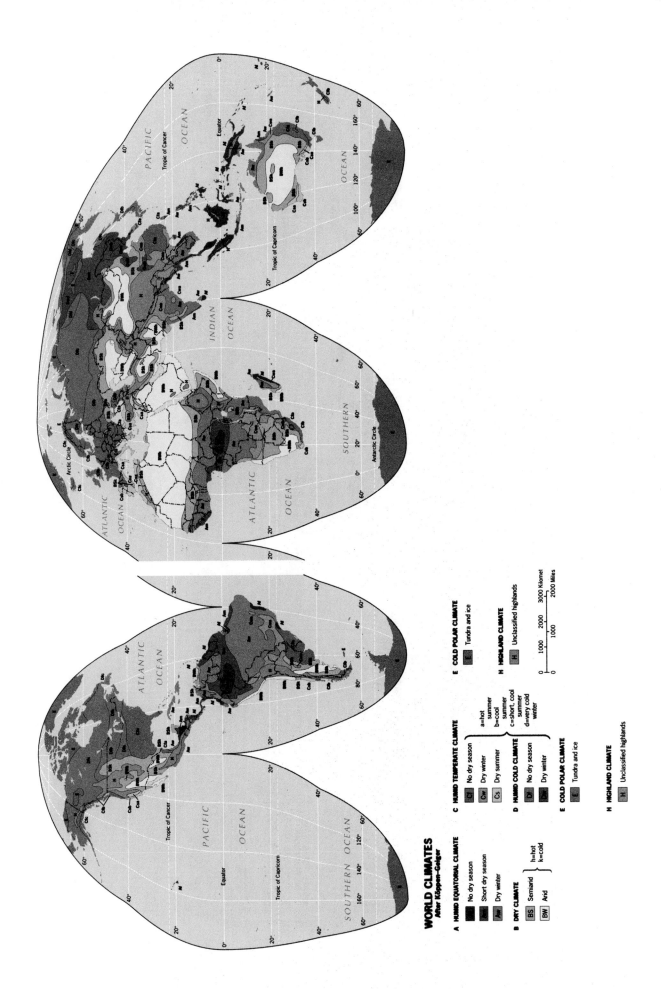

WORLD CLIMATES
After Köppen-Geiger

A HUMID EQUATORIAL CLIMATE
- No dry season
- Short dry season
- **Aw** Dry winter

B DRY CLIMATE
- **BS** Semiarid
- **BW** Arid
  - h=hot
  - k=cold

C HUMID TEMPERATE CLIMATE
- **Cf** No dry season
- **Cw** Dry winter
- **Cs** Dry summer
  - a=hot summer
  - b=cool summer
  - c=short, cool summer
  - d=very cold winter

D HUMID COLD CLIMATE
- **Df** No dry season
- **Dw** Dry winter

E COLD POLAR CLIMATE
- **E** Tundra and ice

H HIGHLAND CLIMATE
- **H** Unclassified highlands

E COLD POLAR CLIMATE
- **E** Tundra and ice

H HIGHLAND CLIMATE
- **H** Unclassified highlands

| 0 | 1000 | 2000 | 3000 Kilomet |
| 0 | 1000 | 2000 Miles |

7

FIGURE I-8

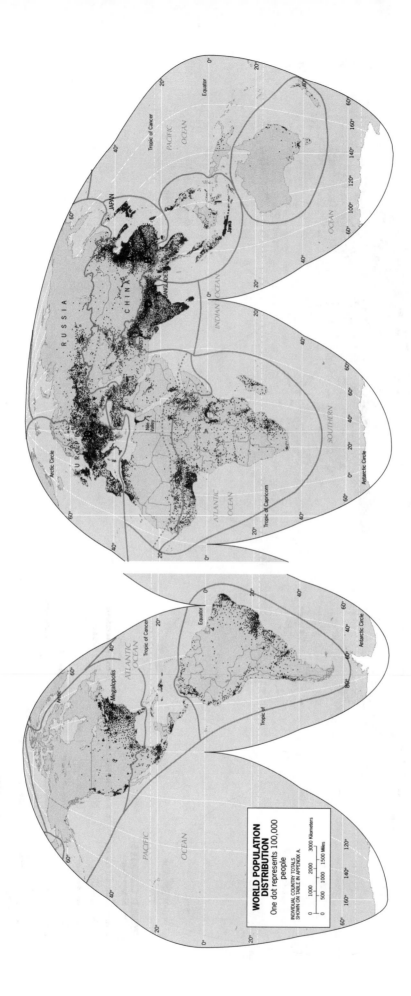

WORLD POPULATION DISTRIBUTION

One dot represents 100,000 people

INDIVIDUAL COUNTRY TOTALS
SHOWN ON TABLE IN APPENDIX A.

0   500   1000   1500 Miles
0   1000   2000   3000 Kilometers

8

FIGURE I-9

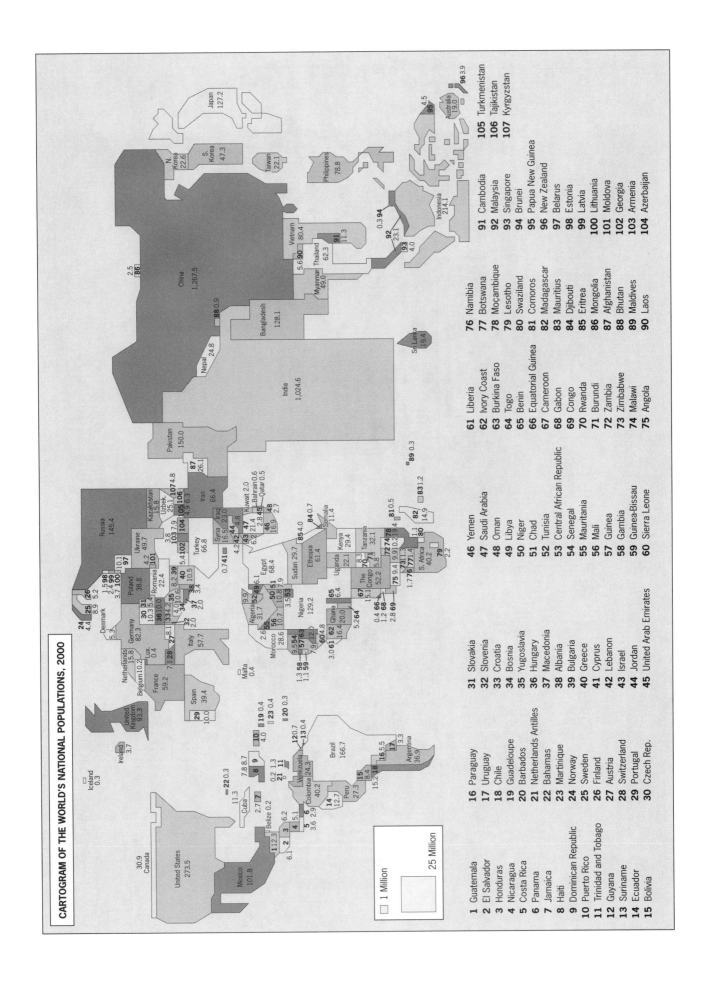

CARTOGRAM OF THE WORLD'S NATIONAL POPULATIONS, 2000

1 Guatemala
2 El Salvador
3 Honduras
4 Nicaragua
5 Costa Rica
6 Panama
7 Jamaica
8 Haiti
9 Dominican Republic
10 Puerto Rico
11 Trinidad and Tobago
12 Guyana
13 Suriname
14 Ecuador
15 Bolivia

16 Paraguay
17 Uruguay
18 Chile
19 Guadeloupe
20 Barbados
21 Netherlands Antilles
22 Bahamas
23 Martinique
24 Norway
25 Sweden
26 Finland
27 Austria
28 Switzerland
29 Portugal
30 Czech Rep.

31 Slovakia
32 Slovenia
33 Croatia
34 Bosnia
35 Yugoslavia
36 Hungary
37 Macedonia
38 Albania
39 Bulgaria
40 Greece
41 Cyprus
42 Lebanon
43 Israel
44 Jordan
45 United Arab Emirates

46 Yemen
47 Saudi Arabia
48 Oman
49 Libya
50 Niger
51 Chad
52 Tunisia
53 Central African Republic
54 Senegal
55 Mauritania
56 Mali
57 Guinea
58 Gambia
59 Guinea-Bissau
60 Sierra Leone

61 Liberia
62 Ivory Coast
63 Burkina Faso
64 Togo
65 Benin
66 Equatorial Guinea
67 Cameroon
68 Gabon
69 Congo
70 Rwanda
71 Burundi
72 Zambia
73 Zimbabwe
74 Malawi
75 Angola

76 Namibia
77 Botswana
78 Moçambique
79 Lesotho
80 Swaziland
81 Comoros
82 Madagascar
83 Mauritius
84 Djibouti
85 Eritrea
86 Mongolia
87 Afghanistan
88 Bhutan
89 Maldives
90 Laos

91 Cambodia
92 Malaysia
93 Singapore
94 Brunei
95 Papua New Guinea
96 New Zealand
97 Belarus
98 Estonia
99 Latvia
100 Lithuania
101 Moldova
102 Georgia
103 Armenia
104 Azerbaijan

105 Turkmenistan
106 Tajikistan
107 Kyrgyzstan

1 Million

25 Million

FIGURE I-10

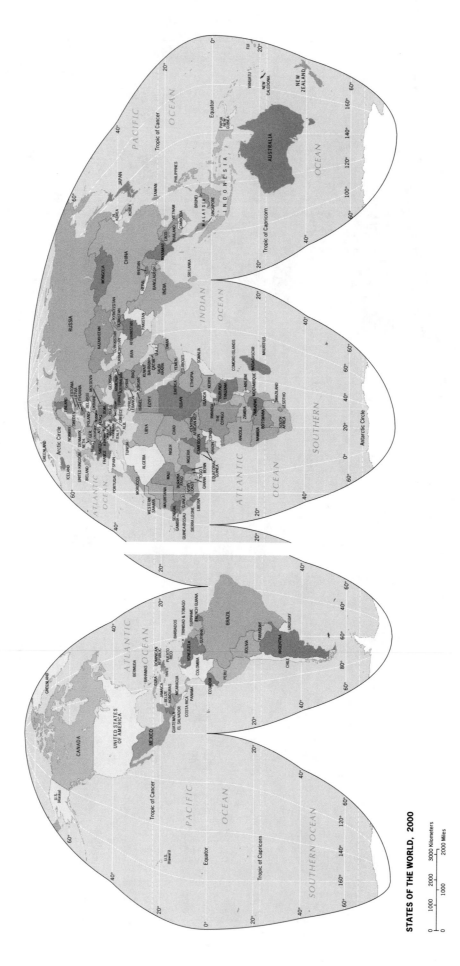

STATES OF THE WORLD, 2000

10

FIGURE I-11

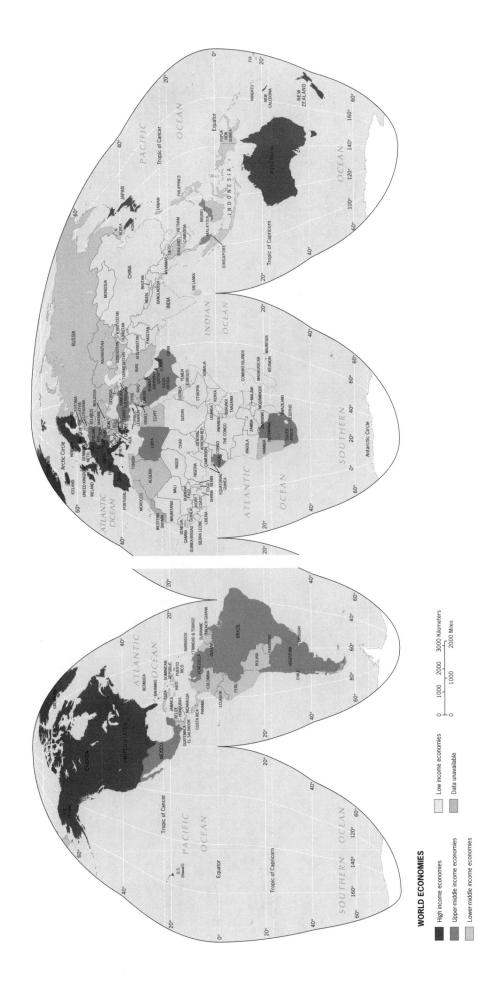

WORLD ECONOMIES

- High income economies
- Upper-middle income economies
- Lower-middle income economies
- Low income economies
- Data unavailable

11

FIGURE I-12

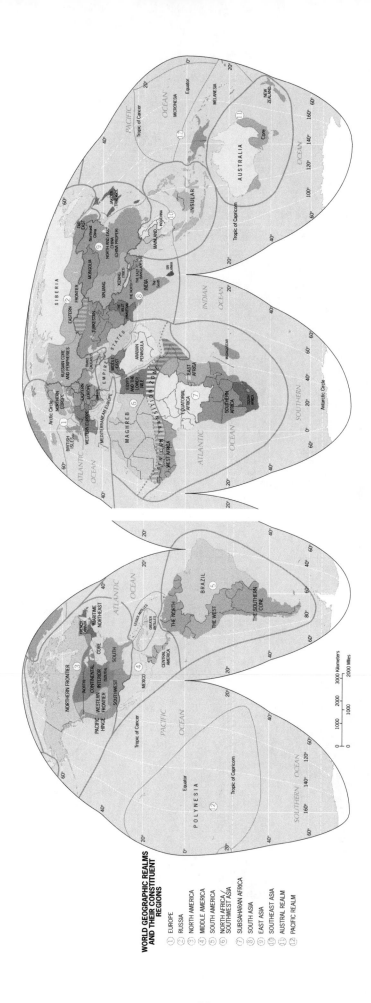

WORLD GEOGRAPHIC REALMS AND THEIR CONSTITUENT REGIONS

1. EUROPE
2. RUSSIA
3. NORTH AMERICA
4. MIDDLE AMERICA
5. SOUTH AMERICA
6. NORTH AFRICA / SOUTHWEST ASIA
7. SUBSAHARAN AFRICA
8. SOUTH ASIA
9. EAST ASIA
10. SOUTHEAST ASIA
11. AUSTRAL REALM
12. PACIFIC REALM

FIGURE I-13

THE RELATIONSHIP BETWEEN
REGIONAL AND SYSTEMATIC GEOGRAPHY

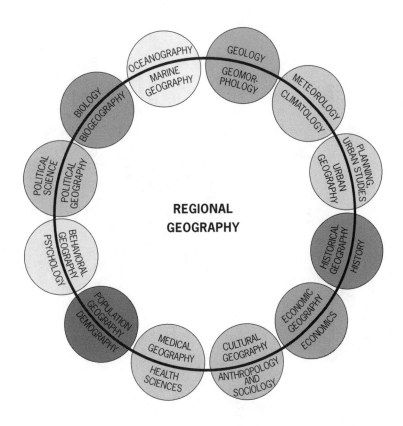

FIGURE I-14

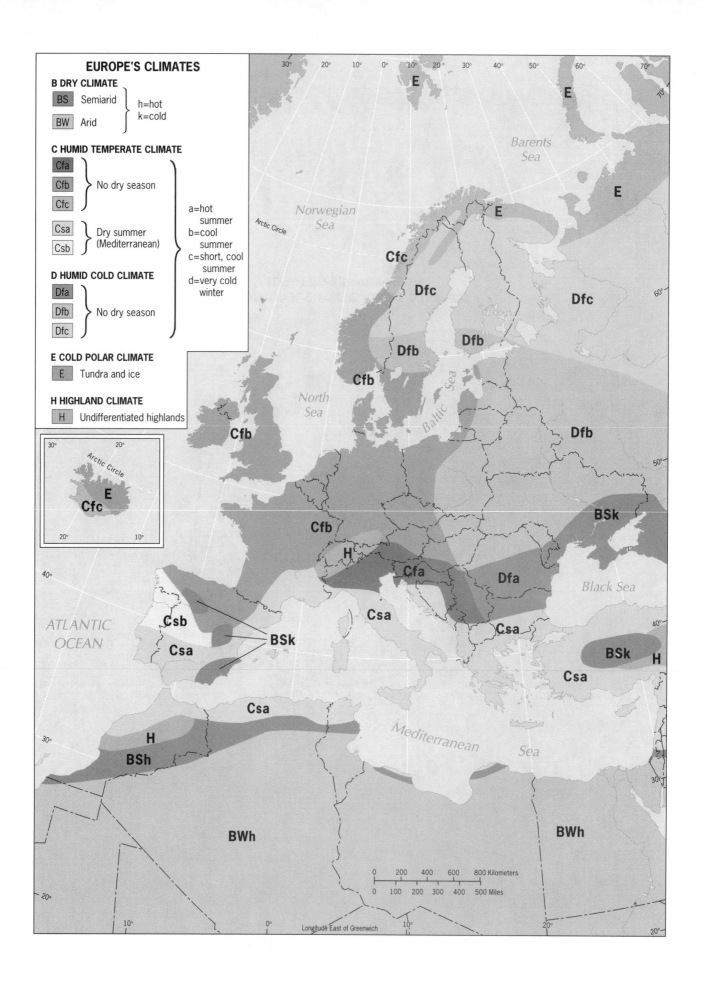

EUROPE'S CLIMATES

B DRY CLIMATE
BS Semiarid
BW Arid
h=hot
k=cold

C HUMID TEMPERATE CLIMATE
Cfa
Cfb   No dry season
Cfc

Csa   Dry summer
Csb   (Mediterranean)

a=hot summer
b=cool summer
c=short, cool summer
d=very cold winter

D HUMID COLD CLIMATE
Dfa
Dfb   No dry season
Dfc

E COLD POLAR CLIMATE
E Tundra and ice

H HIGHLAND CLIMATE
H Undifferentiated highlands

14

FIGURE 1-2

RELATIVE LOCATION: EUROPE IN THE LAND HEMISPHERE

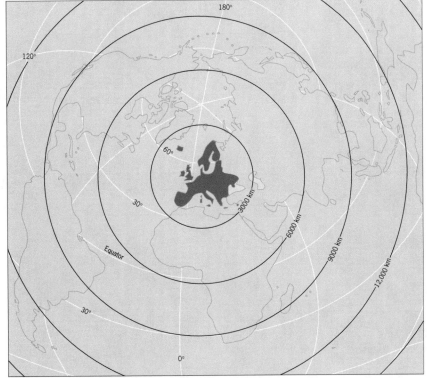

Azimuthal equidistant projection centered on Hamburg, Germany

15   **FIGURE 1-3**

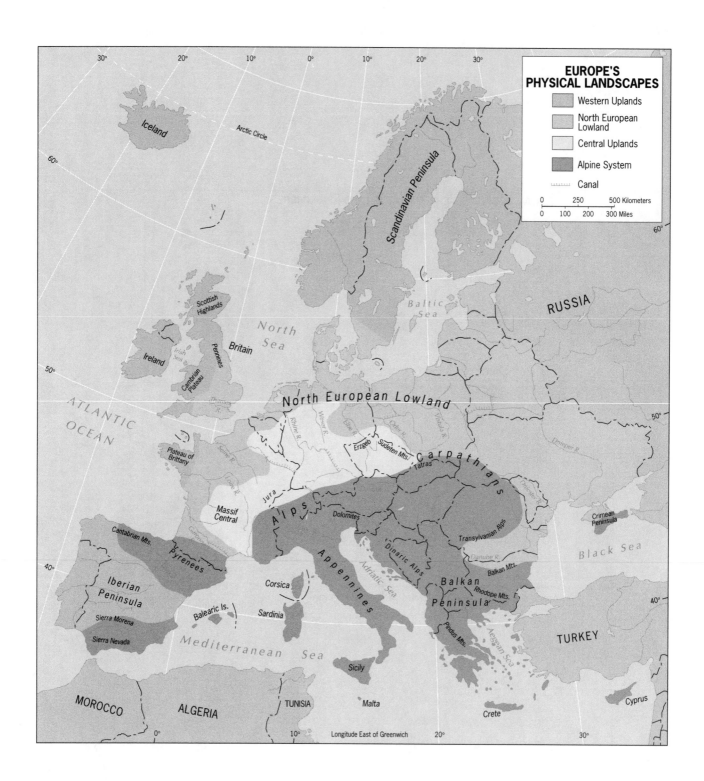

EUROPE'S PHYSICAL LANDSCAPES

Western Uplands

North European Lowland

Central Uplands

Alpine System

Canal

0 250 500 Kilometers

0 100 200 300 Miles

Iceland

Arctic Circle

Scandinavian Peninsula

RUSSIA

Baltic Sea

Scottish Highlands

North Sea

Ireland

Irish Sea

Britain

Pennines

Cambrian Plateau

Thames R.

ATLANTIC OCEAN

North European Lowland

Rhine R.

Weser R.

Elbe

Oder R.

Vistula R.

Dnieper R.

Plateau of Brittany

Seine R.

Erzgeb.

Sudeten Mts.

Carpathians

Loire R.

Jura

Tatras

Massif Central

Alps

Dolomites

Transylvanian Alps

Dniester R.

Crimean Peninsula

Cantabrian Mts.

Pyrenees

Appennines

Dinaric Alps

Adriatic Sea

Danube R.

Black Sea

Iberian Peninsula

Corsica

Balkan Peninsula

Balkan Mts.

Sierra Morena

Balearic Is.

Sardinia

Rhodope Mts.

Sierra Nevada

Mediterranean Sea

Pindus Mts.

Aegean Sea

TURKEY

Sicily

MOROCCO

ALGERIA

TUNISIA

Malta

Crete

Cyprus

Longitude East of Greenwich

16

FIGURE 1-4

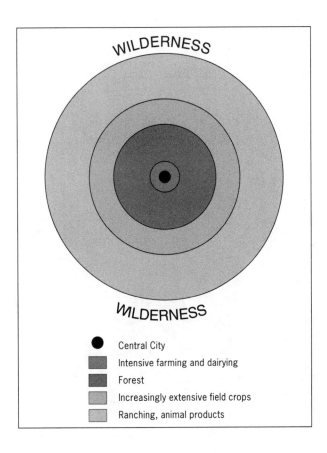

Central City

Intensive farming and dairying

Forest

Increasingly extensive field crops

Ranching, animal products

17

FIGURE 1-5

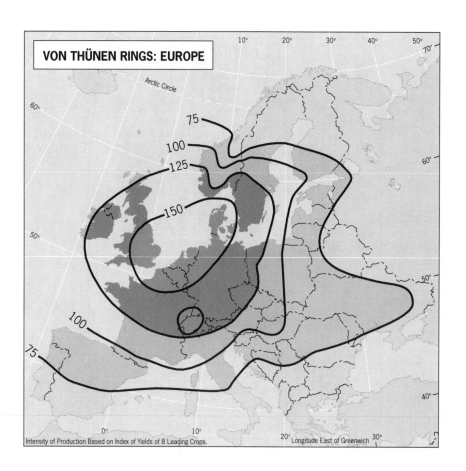

VON THÜNEN RINGS: EUROPE

Intensity of Production Based on Index of Yields of 8 Leading Crops.

Longitude East of Greenwich

18

FIGURE 1-6

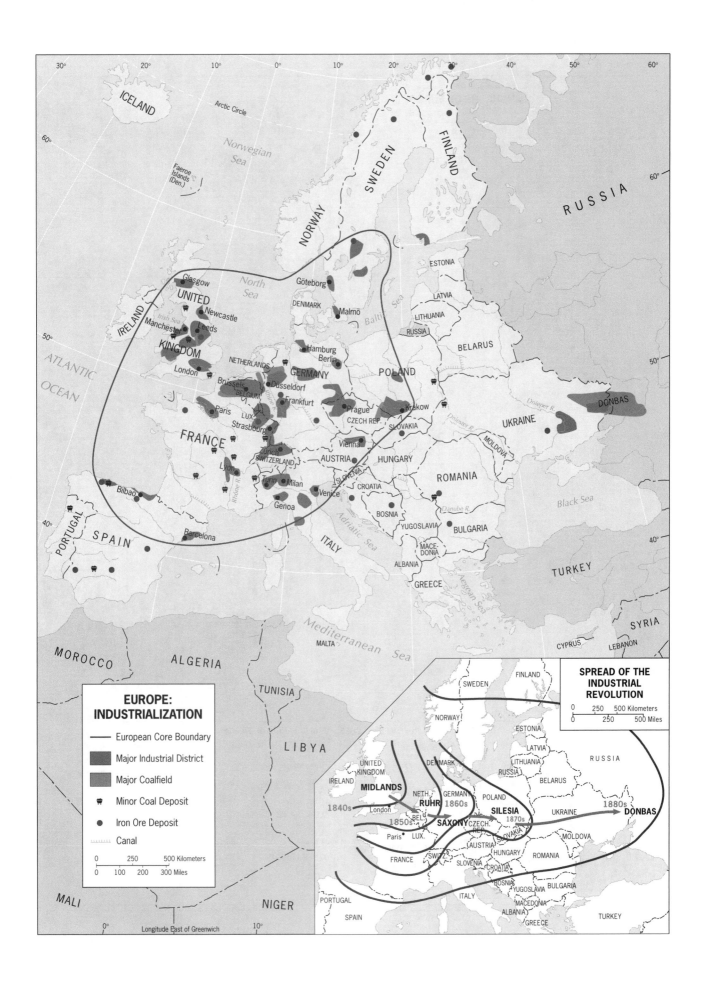

19

FIGURE 1-7

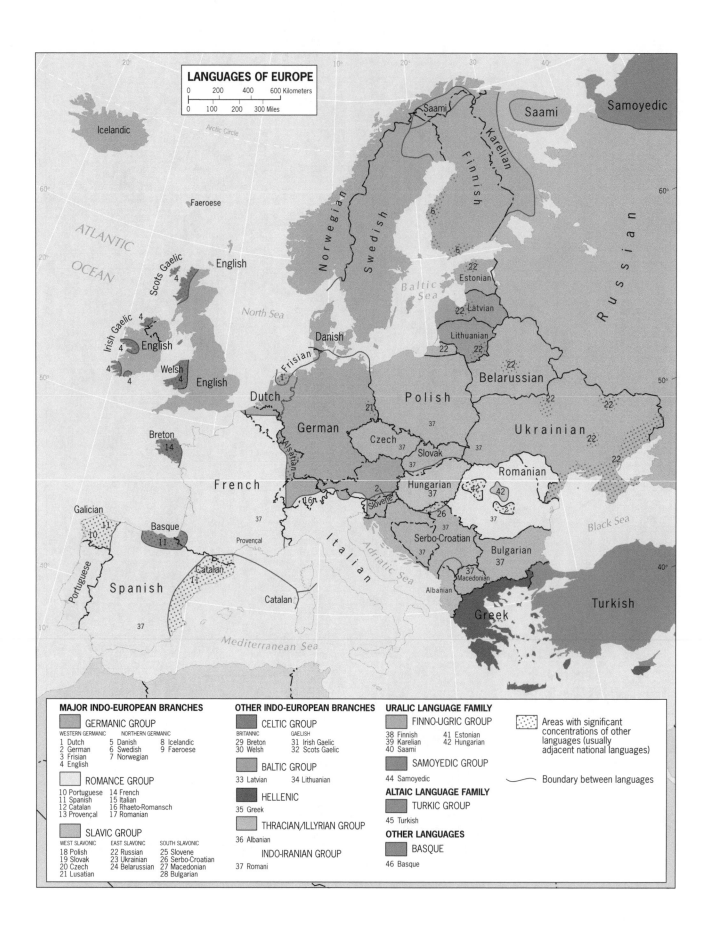

LANGUAGES OF EUROPE

0   200   400   600 Kilometers
0   100   200   300 Miles

MAJOR INDO-EUROPEAN BRANCHES

GERMANIC GROUP

WESTERN GERMANIC	NORTHERN GERMANIC	
1 Dutch	5 Danish	8 Icelandic
2 German	6 Swedish	9 Faeroese
3 Frisian	7 Norwegian	
4 English		

ROMANCE GROUP

10 Portuguese	14 French
11 Spanish	15 Italian
12 Catalan	16 Rhaeto-Romansch
13 Provençal	17 Romanian

SLAVIC GROUP

WEST SLAVONIC	EAST SLAVONIC	SOUTH SLAVONIC
18 Polish	22 Russian	25 Slovene
19 Slovak	23 Ukrainian	26 Serbo-Croatian
20 Czech	24 Belarussian	27 Macedonian
21 Lusatian		28 Bulgarian

OTHER INDO-EUROPEAN BRANCHES

CELTIC GROUP

BRITANNIC	GAELISH
29 Breton	31 Irish Gaelic
30 Welsh	32 Scots Gaelic

BALTIC GROUP

33 Latvian	34 Lithuanian

HELLENIC GROUP

35 Greek

THRACIAN/ILLYRIAN GROUP

36 Albanian

INDO-IRANIAN GROUP

37 Romani

URALIC LANGUAGE FAMILY

FINNO-UGRIC GROUP

38 Finnish	41 Estonian
39 Karelian	42 Hungarian
40 Saami	

SAMOYEDIC GROUP

44 Samoyedic

ALTAIC LANGUAGE FAMILY

TURKIC GROUP

45 Turkish

OTHER LANGUAGES

BASQUE

46 Basque

Areas with significant concentrations of other languages (usually adjacent national languages)

Boundary between languages

FIGURE 1-8

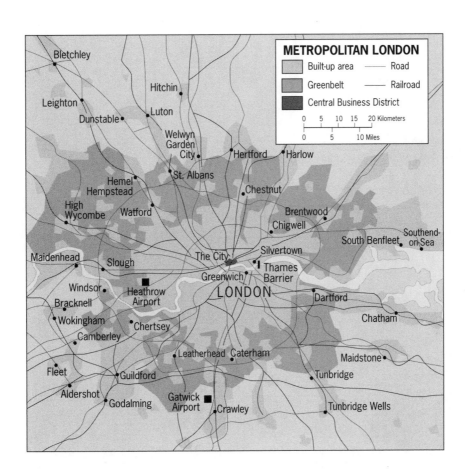

FIGURE 1-9

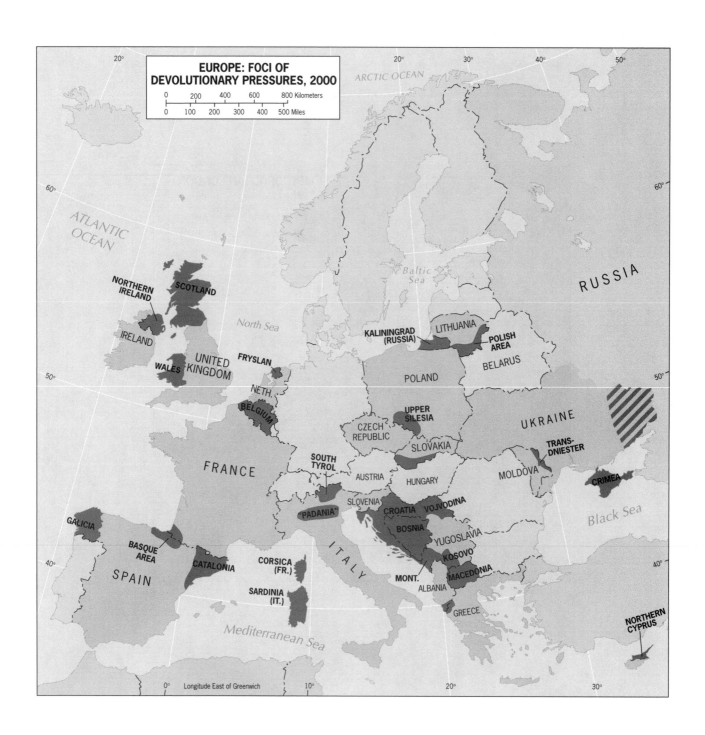

EUROPE: FOCI OF DEVOLUTIONARY PRESSURES, 2000

FIGURE 1-10

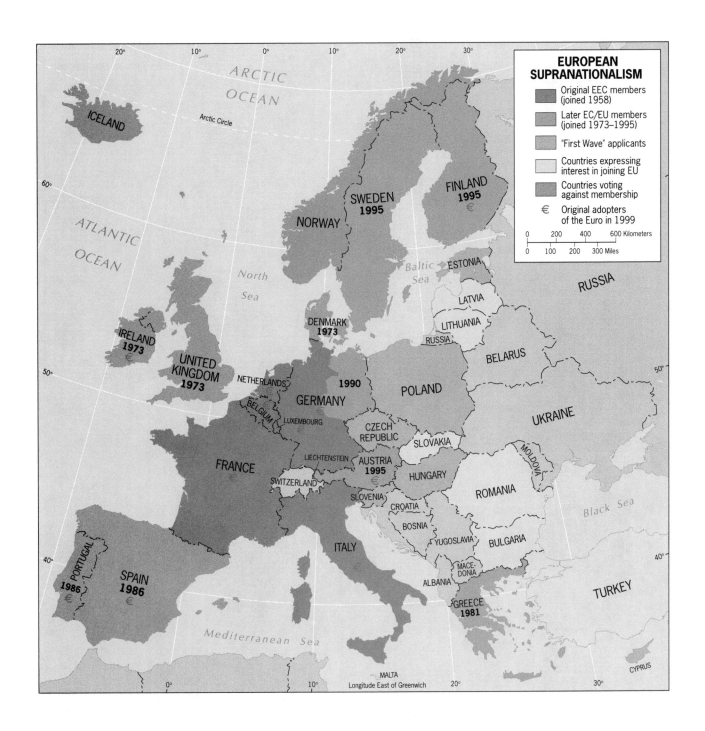

EUROPEAN SUPRANATIONALISM

- Original EEC members (joined 1958)
- Later EC/EU members (joined 1973–1995)
- "First Wave" applicants
- Countries expressing interest in joining EU
- Countries voting against membership
- € Original adopters of the Euro in 1999

0 200 400 600 Kilometers
0 100 200 300 Miles

23

FIGURE 1-11

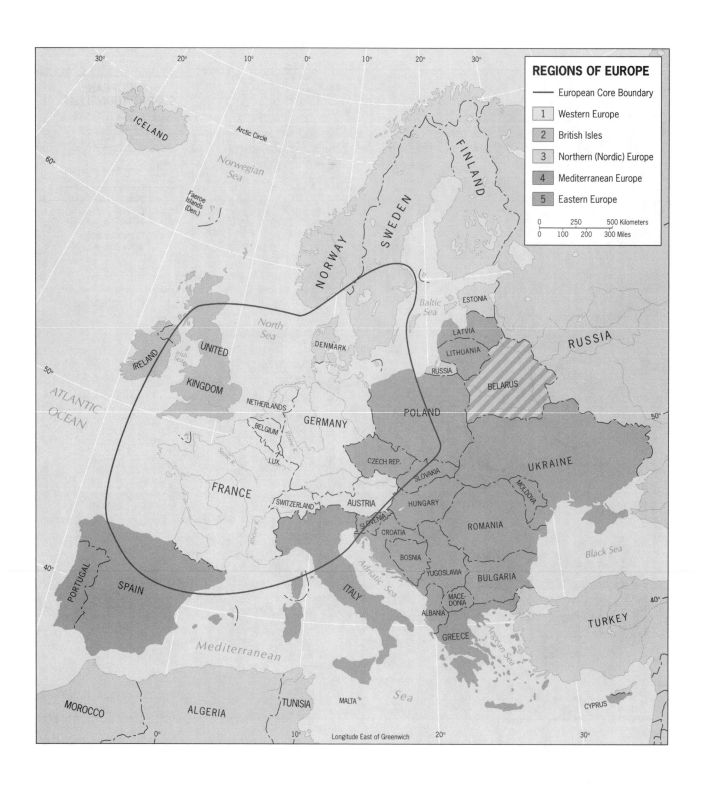

REGIONS OF EUROPE

—— European Core Boundary

1   Western Europe
2   British Isles
3   Northern (Nordic) Europe
4   Mediterranean Europe
5   Eastern Europe

0   250   500 Kilometers
0   100   200   300 Miles

Longitude East of Greenwich

FIGURE 1-12

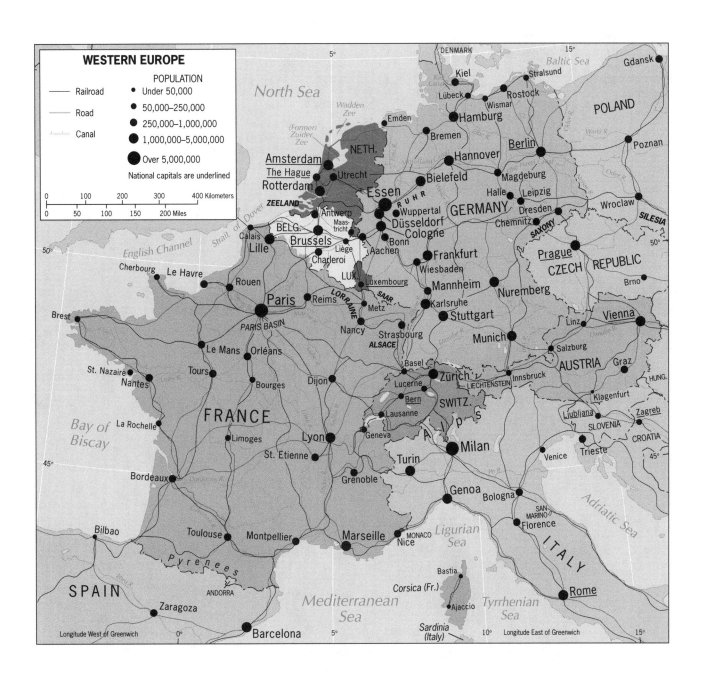

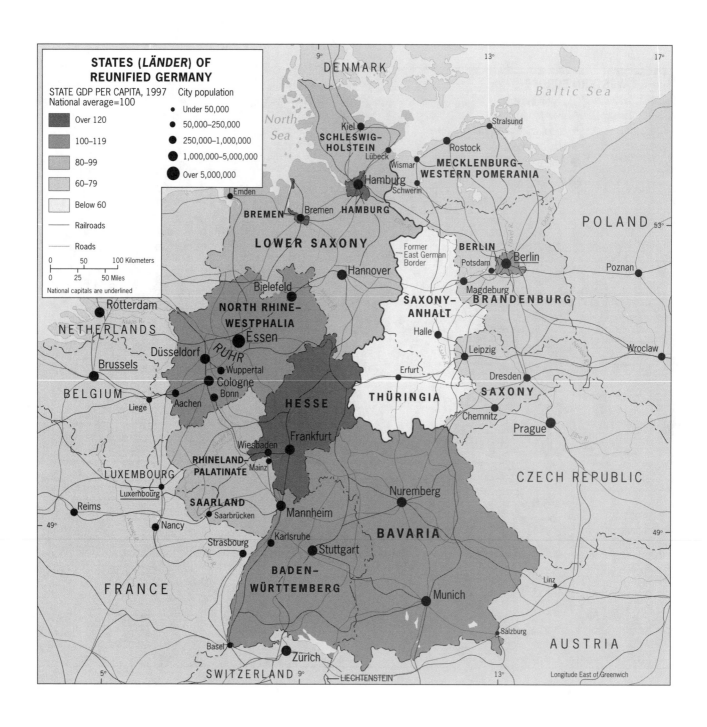

STATES (*LÄNDER*) OF
REUNIFIED GERMANY

STATE GDP PER CAPITA, 1997   City population
National average=100

- Over 120
- 100–119
- 80–99
- 60–79
- Below 60
- Railroads
- Roads

City population
- Under 50,000
- 50,000–250,000
- 250,000–1,000,000
- 1,000,000–5,000,000
- Over 5,000,000

0   50   100 Kilometers
0   25   50 Miles

National capitals are underlined

26

FIGURE 1-14

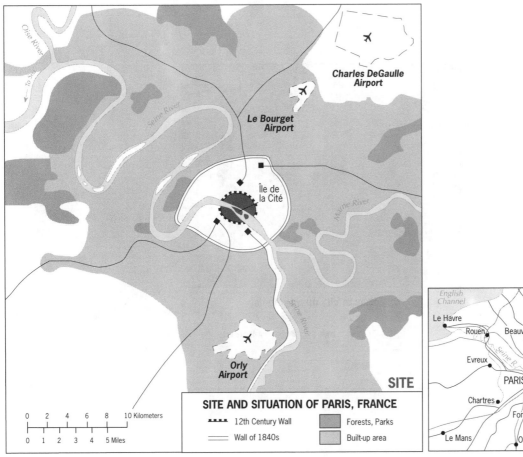

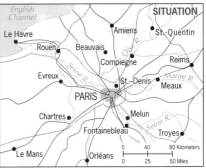

SITE AND SITUATION OF PARIS, FRANCE

▪▪▪▪ 12th Century Wall

⎯⎯⎯ Wall of 1840s

Forests, Parks

Built-up area

SITE

SITUATION

27

FIGURE 1-15

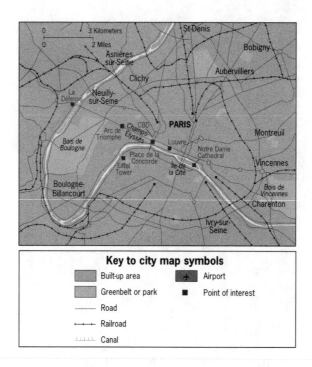

Key to city map symbols

Built-up area

Greenbelt or park

Road

Railroad

Canal

✈ Airport

■ Point of interest

PARIS

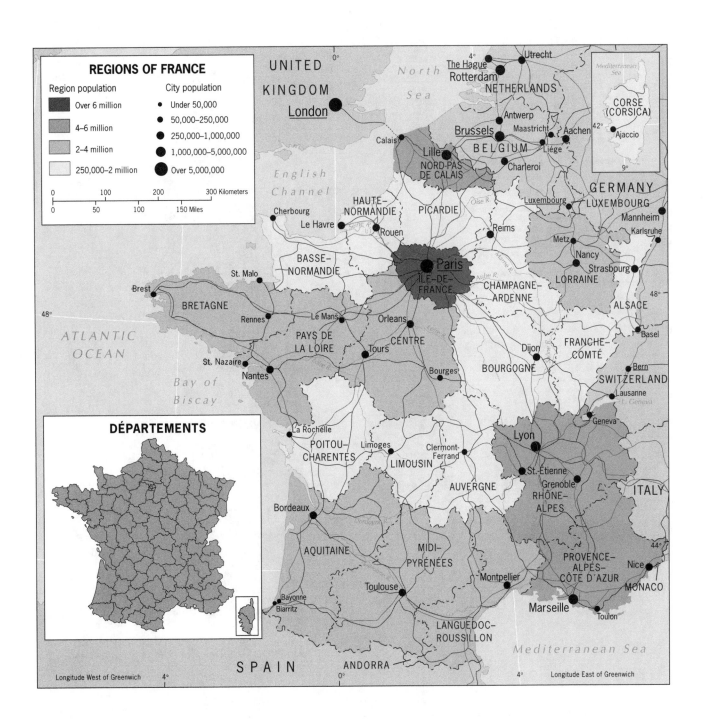

REGIONS OF FRANCE

Region population | City population
Over 6 million | Under 50,000
4–6 million | 50,000–250,000
2–4 million | 250,000–1,000,000
250,000–2 million | 1,000,000–5,000,000
 | Over 5,000,000

0   100   200   300 Kilometers
0   50   100   150 Miles

DÉPARTEMENTS

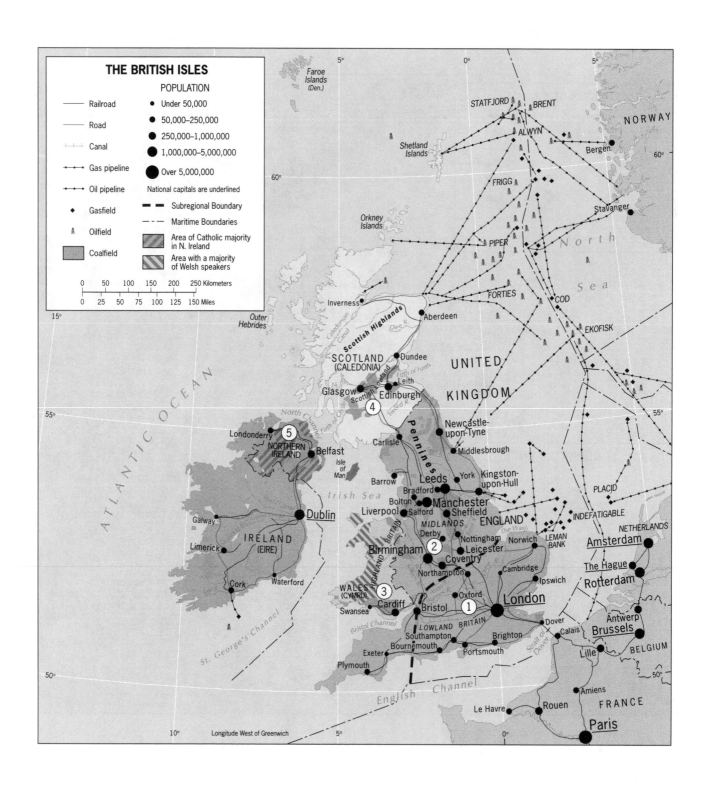

THE BRITISH ISLES

POPULATION

Railroad	• Under 50,000
Road	• 50,000–250,000
Canal	● 250,000–1,000,000
Gas pipeline	● 1,000,000–5,000,000
Oil pipeline	● Over 5,000,000
Gasfield	National capitals are underlined
Oilfield	▬ ▬ Subregional Boundary
Coalfield	—·— Maritime Boundaries

Area of Catholic majority in N. Ireland

Area with a majority of Welsh speakers

0 50 100 150 200 250 Kilometers

0 25 50 75 100 125 150 Miles

FIGURE 1-17

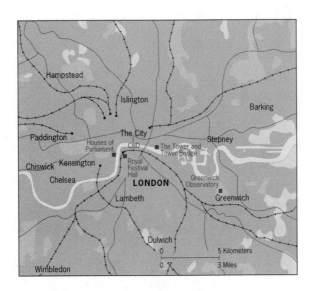

LONDON

NORTHERN (NORDIC) EUROPE

POPULATION

Railroad

Road

Gasfield

Gas pipeline

Oilfield

Oil pipeline

- Under 50,000
- 50,000–250,000
- 250,000–1,000,000
- 1,000,000–5,000,000
- Over 5,000,000

National capitals are underlined

Core area

| 0 | 100 | 200 | 300 | 400 Kilometers |
| 0 | 50 | 100 | 150 | 200 | 250 Miles |

FIGURE 1-18

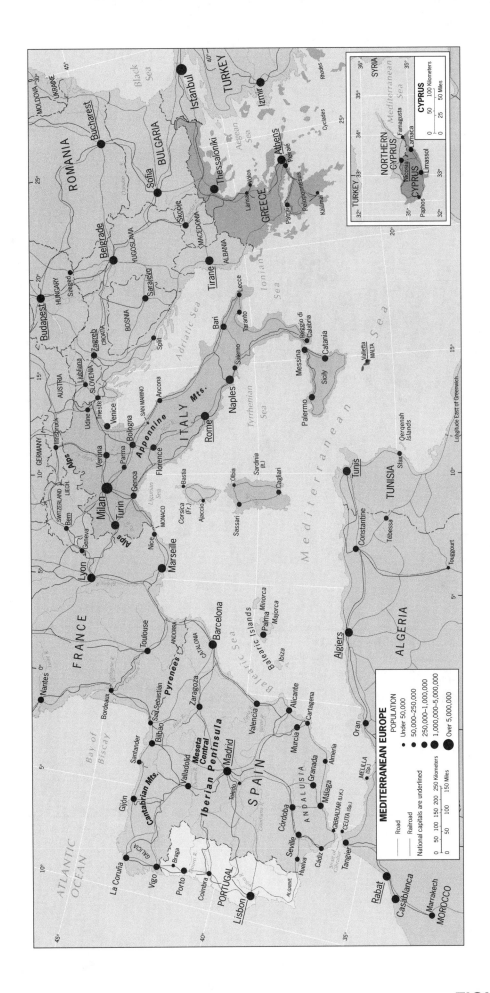

33

FIGURE 1-19

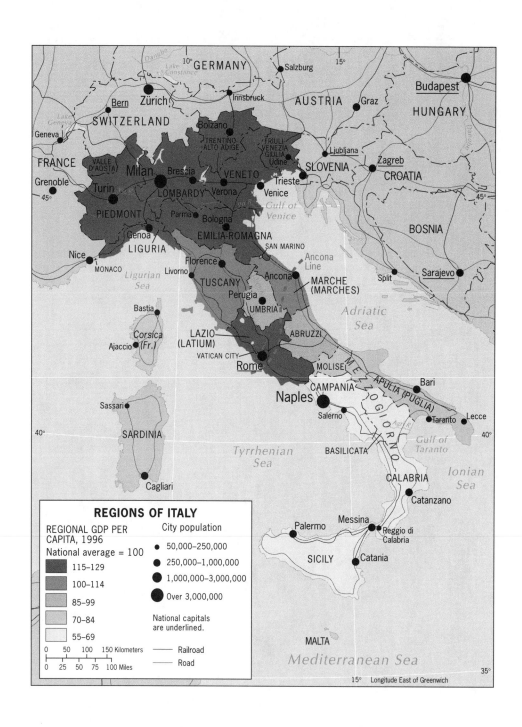

REGIONS OF ITALY

REGIONAL GDP PER CAPITA, 1996
National average = 100

- 115–129
- 100–114
- 85–99
- 70–84
- 55–69

City population
- ● 50,000–250,000
- ● 250,000–1,000,000
- ● 1,000,000–3,000,000
- ● Over 3,000,000

National capitals are underlined.

0   50   100   150 Kilometers
0   25   50   75   100 Miles

—— Railroad
—— Road

FIGURE 1-20

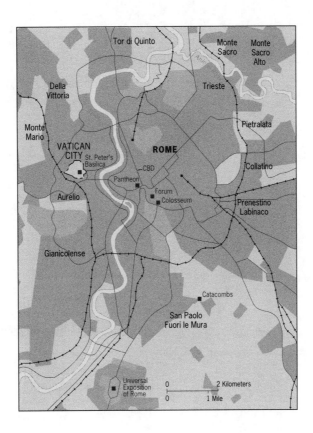

35

ROME

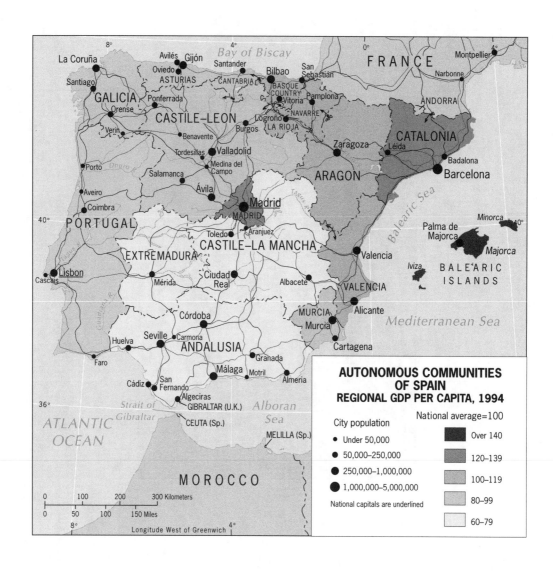

AUTONOMOUS COMMUNITIES OF SPAIN
REGIONAL GDP PER CAPITA, 1994

National average=100

City population
- Under 50,000
- 50,000–250,000
- 250,000–1,000,000
- 1,000,000–5,000,000

National capitals are underlined

Over 140
120–139
100–119
80–99
60–79

FIGURE 1-21

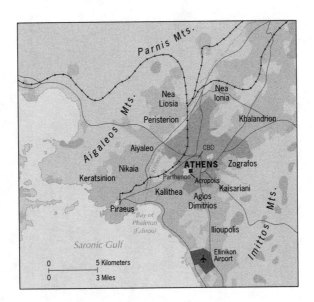

FORMER EASTERN EUROPE (1919–1991)

POPULATION
- Under 50,000
- 50,000–250,000
- 250,000–1,000,000
- 1,000,000–5,000,000
- Over 5,000,000

National capitals are underlined

FORMER YUGOSLAVIA:
- Albanians
- Croats
- Hungarians
- Macedonians
- Montenegrins
- Serbs
- Slovenes

- **B** Bulgarians
- **H** Hungarians
- **I** Italians
- **R** Romanians
- **T** Turks
- Railroad
- Pre-World War II boundary

0 50 100 150 Kilometers
0 25 50 75 Miles

THE NEW EASTERN EUROPE

POPULATION

- Under 50,000
- 50,000–250,000
- 250,000–1,000,000
- 1,000,000–5,000,000
- Over 5,000,000

— Road
— Railroad

National capitals are underlined

Soviet-era realm boundary

Present realm boundary

0 100 200 300 400 Kilometers
0 50 100 150 200 Miles

Longitude East of Greenwich

FIGURE 1-23

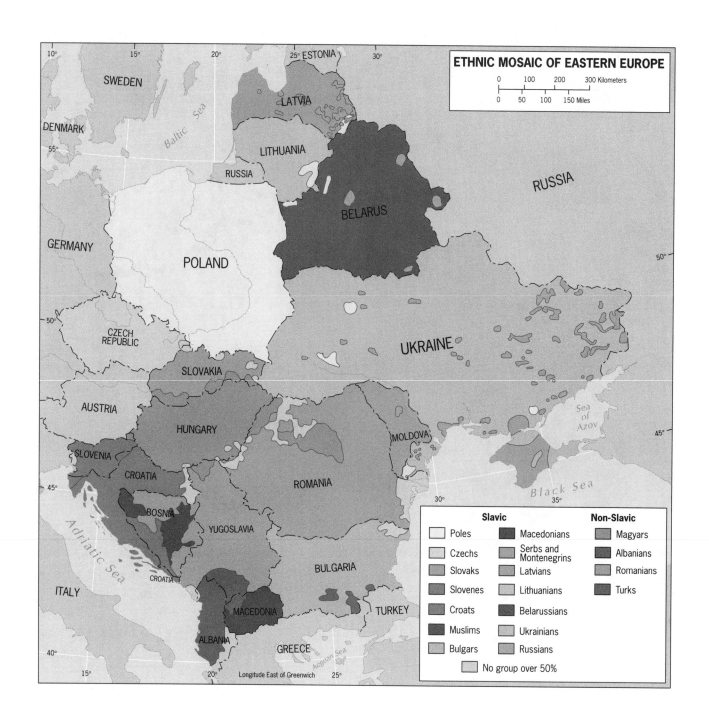

ETHNIC MOSAIC OF EASTERN EUROPE

Slavic		Non-Slavic
Poles	Macedonians	Magyars
Czechs	Serbs and Montenegrins	Albanians
Slovaks	Latvians	Romanians
Slovenes	Lithuanians	Turks
Croats	Belarussians	
Muslims	Ukrainians	
Bulgars	Russians	
	No group over 50%	

FIGURE 1-24

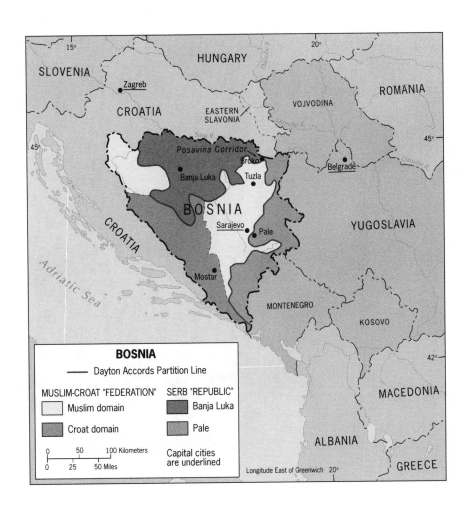

BOSNIA

— Dayton Accords Partition Line

MUSLIM-CROAT "FEDERATION"
- Muslim domain
- Croat domain

SERB "REPUBLIC"
- Banja Luka
- Pale

0   50   100 Kilometers
0   25   50 Miles

Capital cities are underlined

Longitude East of Greenwich 20°

41

FIGURE 1-25

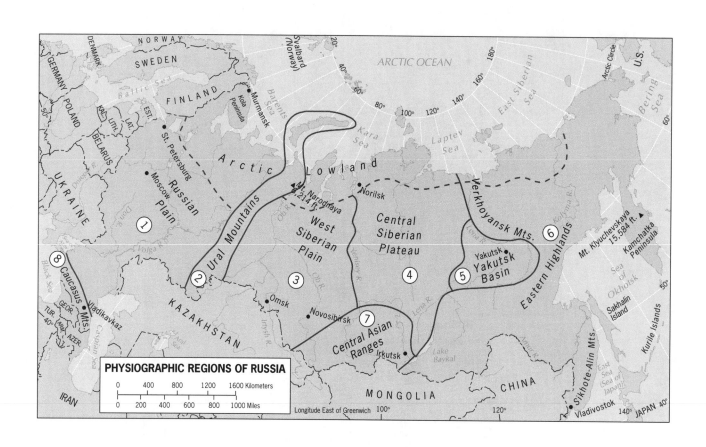

PHYSIOGRAPHIC REGIONS OF RUSSIA

0   400   800   1200   1600 Kilometers

0   200   400   600   800   1000 Miles

FIGURE 2-2

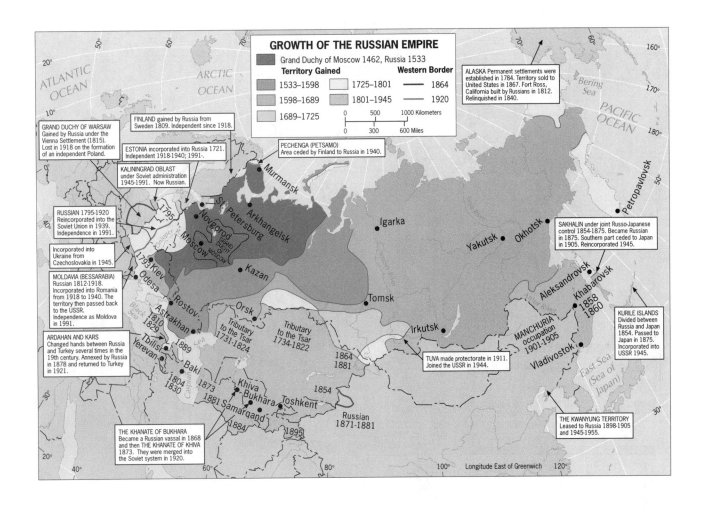

GROWTH OF THE RUSSIAN EMPIRE

Legend:
- Grand Duchy of Moscow 1462, Russia 1533

Territory Gained
- 1533–1598
- 1598–1689
- 1689–1725
- 1725–1801
- 1801–1945

Western Border
- —— 1864
- ···· 1920

0 500 1000 Kilometers
0 300 600 Miles

ALASKA Permanent settlements were established in 1784. Territory sold to United States in 1867. Fort Ross, California built by Russians in 1812. Relinquished in 1840.

GRAND DUCHY OF WARSAW Gained by Russia under the Vienna Settlement (1815). Lost in 1918 on the formation of an independent Poland.

FINLAND gained by Russia from Sweden 1809. Independent since 1918.

ESTONIA incorporated into Russia 1721. Independent 1918-1940; 1991-.

KALININGRAD OBLAST under Soviet administration 1945-1991. Now Russian.

PECHENGA (PETSAMO) Area ceded by Finland to Russia in 1940.

RUSSIAN 1795-1920 Reincorporated into the Soviet Union in 1939. Independence in 1991.

SAKHALIN under joint Russo-Japanese control 1854-1875. Became Russian in 1875. Southern part ceded to Japan in 1905. Reincorporated 1945.

Incorporated into Ukraine from Czechoslovakia in 1945.

MOLDAVIA (BESSARABIA) Russian 1812-1918. Incorporated into Romania from 1918 to 1940. The territory then passed back to the USSR. Independence as Moldova in 1991.

KURILE ISLANDS Divided between Russia and Japan 1854. Passed to Japan in 1875. Incorporated into USSR 1945.

ARDAHAN AND KARS Changed hands between Russia and Turkey several times in the 19th century. Annexed by Russia in 1878 and returned to Turkey in 1921.

TUVA made protectorate in 1911. Joined the USSR in 1944.

THE KWANYUNG TERRITORY Leased to Russia 1898-1905 and 1945-1955.

THE KHANATE OF BUKHARA Became a Russian vassal in 1868 and then THE KHANATE OF KHIVA 1873. They were merged into the Soviet system in 1920.

Tributary to the Tsar 1731-1824

Tributary to the Tsar 1734-1822

Russian 1871-1881

Murmansk · Arkhangelsk · St. Petersburg · Novgorod · Moscow · Kazan · Igarka · Yakutsk · Okhotsk · Petropavlovsk · Tomsk · Irkutsk · Aleksandrovsk · Khabarovsk 1858 1860 · Vladivostok · Orsk · Astrakhan · Odesa · Rostov · Kiev 1793 · Tbilisi · Yerevan · Baki · Khiva · Bukhara · Toshkent · Samarqand · MANCHURIA occupation 1901-1905

ATLANTIC OCEAN · ARCTIC OCEAN · PACIFIC OCEAN · Bering Sea · Black Sea · Caspian Sea · East Sea (Sea of Japan)

43

FIGURE 2-3

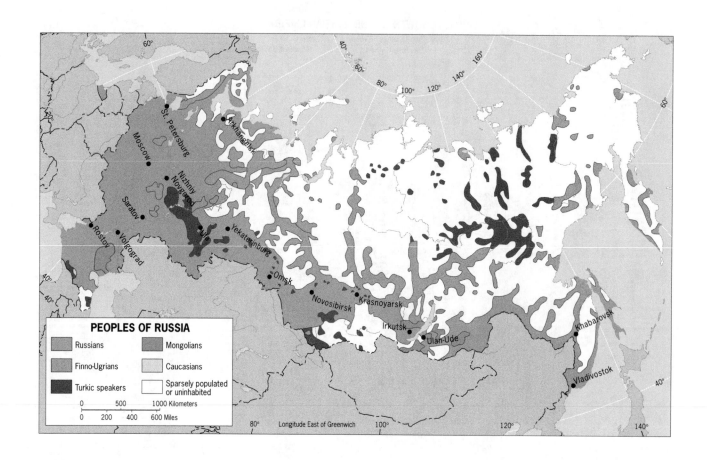

PEOPLES OF RUSSIA

- Russians
- Finno-Ugrians
- Turkic speakers
- Mongolians
- Caucasians
- Sparsely populated or uninhabited

0 500 1000 Kilometers
0 200 400 600 Miles

Longitude East of Greenwich

FIGURE 2-4

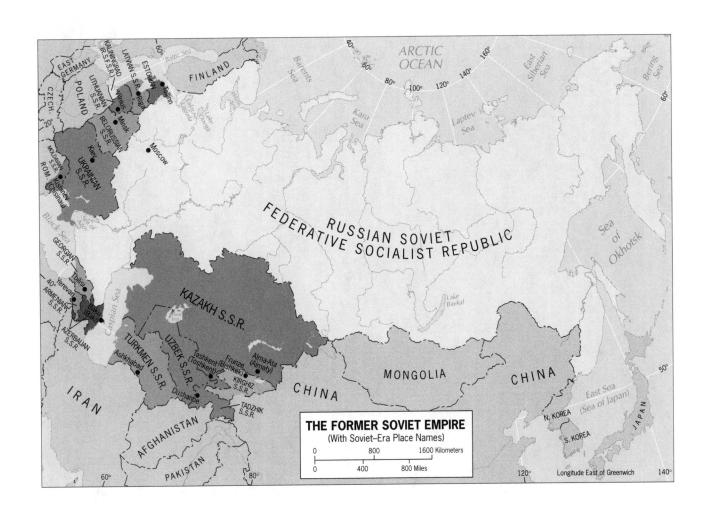

THE FORMER SOVIET EMPIRE
(With Soviet–Era Place Names)

0   800   1600 Kilometers

0   400   800 Miles

FIGURE 2-5

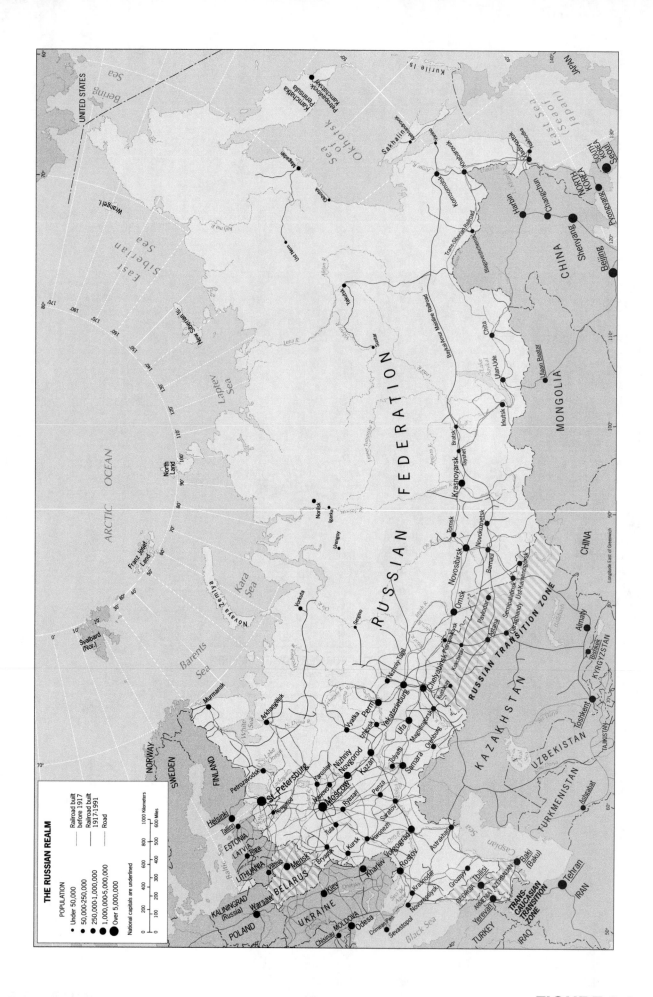

46

FIGURE 2-6

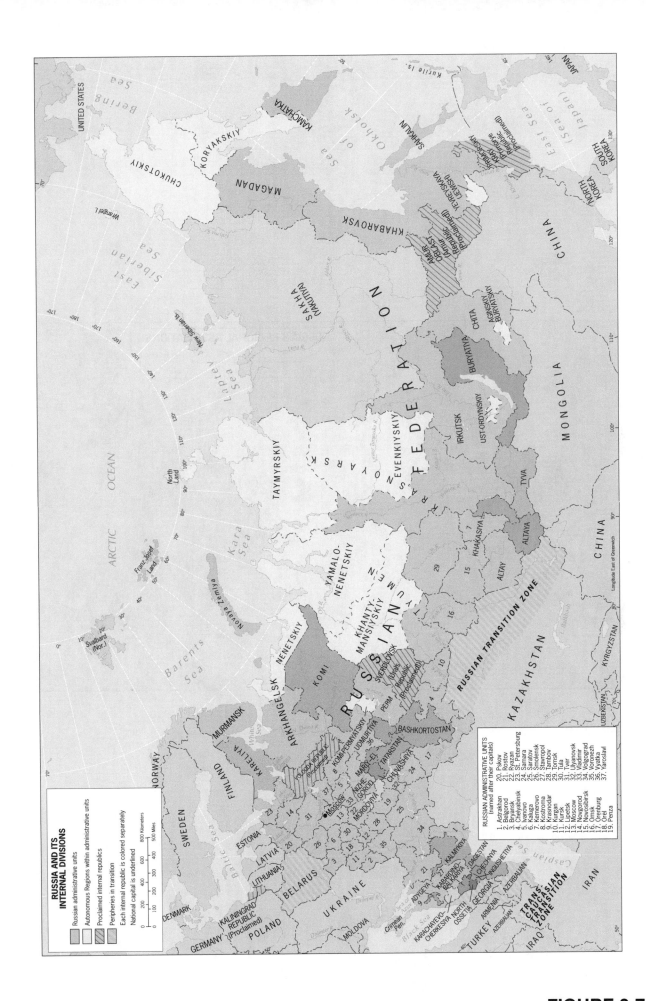

RUSSIA AND ITS INTERNAL DIVISIONS

Russian administrative units

Autonomous Regions within administrative units

Proclaimed internal republics

Peripheries in transition

Each internal republic is colored separately

National capital is underlined

0   100   200   300   400   500 Miles
0   200   400   600   800 Kilometers

RUSSIAN ADMINISTRATIVE UNITS
(named after their capitals)

1. Astrakhan
2. Belgorod
3. Bryansk
4. Chelyabinsk
5. Ivanovo
6. Kaluga
7. Kemerovo
8. Kostroma
9. Krasnodar
10. Kurgan
11. Kursk
12. Lipetsk
13. Moscow
14. Novgorod
15. Novosibirsk
16. Omsk
17. Orenburg
18. Orel
19. Penza
20. Pskov
21. Rostov
22. Ryazan
23. St. Petersburg
24. Samara
25. Saratov
26. Smolensk
27. Stavropol
28. Tambov
29. Tomsk
30. Tula
31. Tver
32. Ulyanovsk
33. Vladimir
34. Volgograd
35. Voronezh
36. Vyatka
37. Yaroslavl

FIGURE 2-7

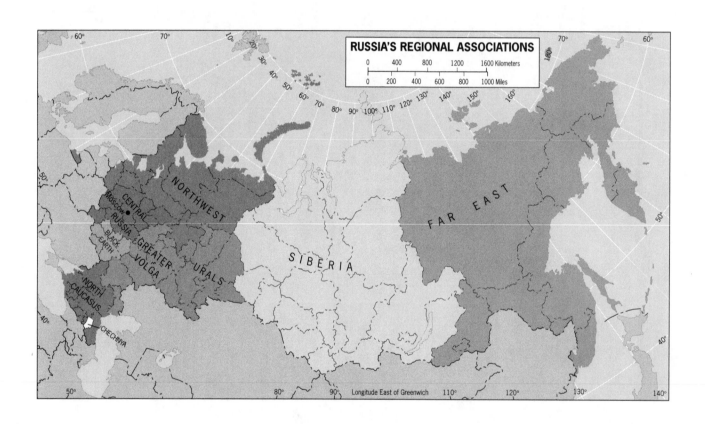

RUSSIA'S REGIONAL ASSOCIATIONS

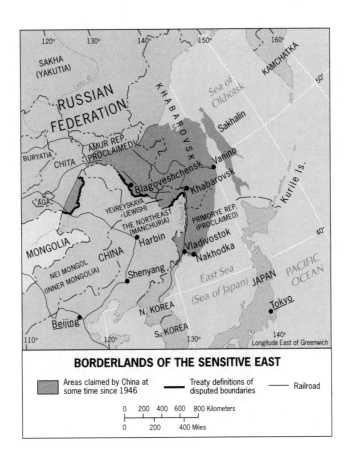

BORDERLANDS OF THE SENSITIVE EAST

Areas claimed by China at some time since 1946 — Treaty definitions of disputed boundaries — Railroad

0 200 400 600 800 Kilometers

0 200 400 Miles

49

FIGURE 2-9

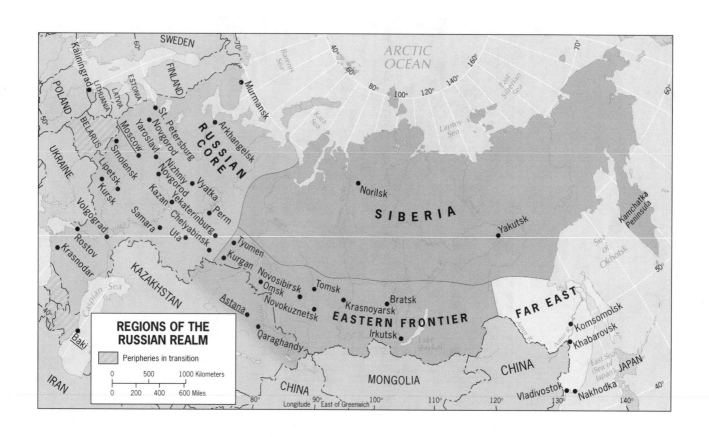

FIGURE 2-10

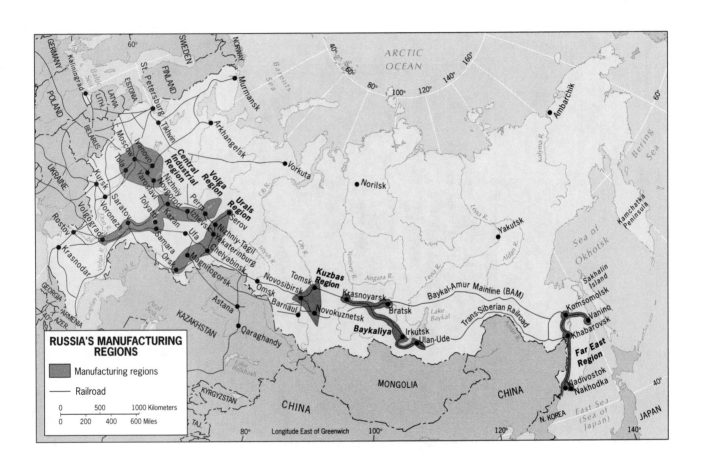

RUSSIA'S MANUFACTURING REGIONS

- Manufacturing regions
- Railroad

```
0        500        1000 Kilometers
0   200   400   600 Miles
```

FIGURE 2-11

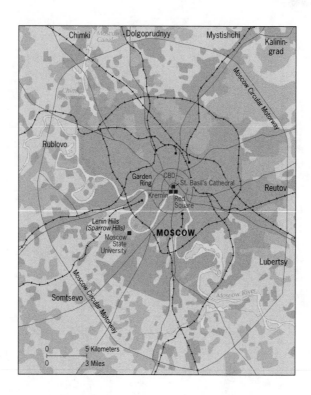

Chimki
Dolgoprudnyy
Mystishchi
Kalinin-
grad

Moscow
Canal

Moscow Circular Motorway

Rublovo

Garden
Ring

CBD

St. Basil's Cathedral

Reutov

Kremlin

Red
Square

Lenin Hills
(Sparrow Hills)

MOSCOW

Moscow
State
University

Lubertsy

Moscow River

Somtsevo

Moscow Circular Motorway

0   5 Kilometers

0   3 Miles

MOSCOW

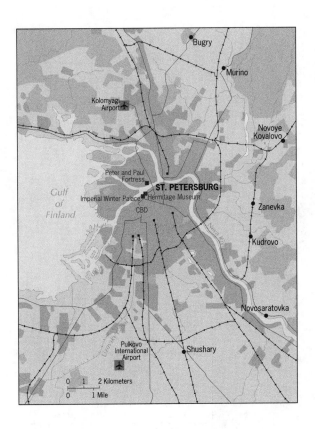

ST. PETERSBURG

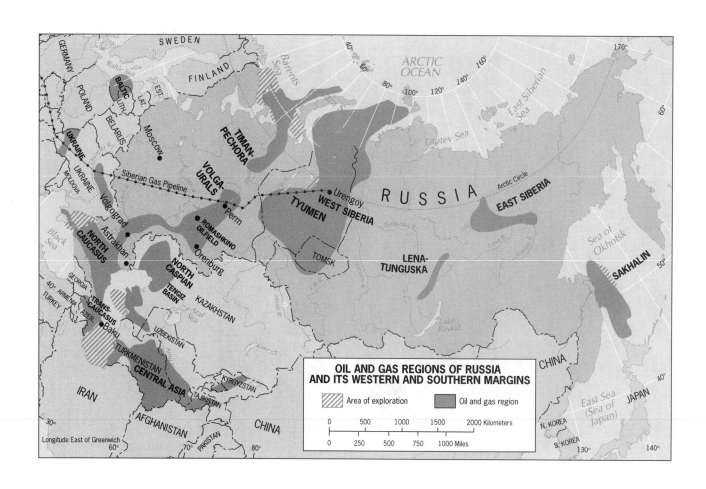

OIL AND GAS REGIONS OF RUSSIA
AND ITS WESTERN AND SOUTHERN MARGINS

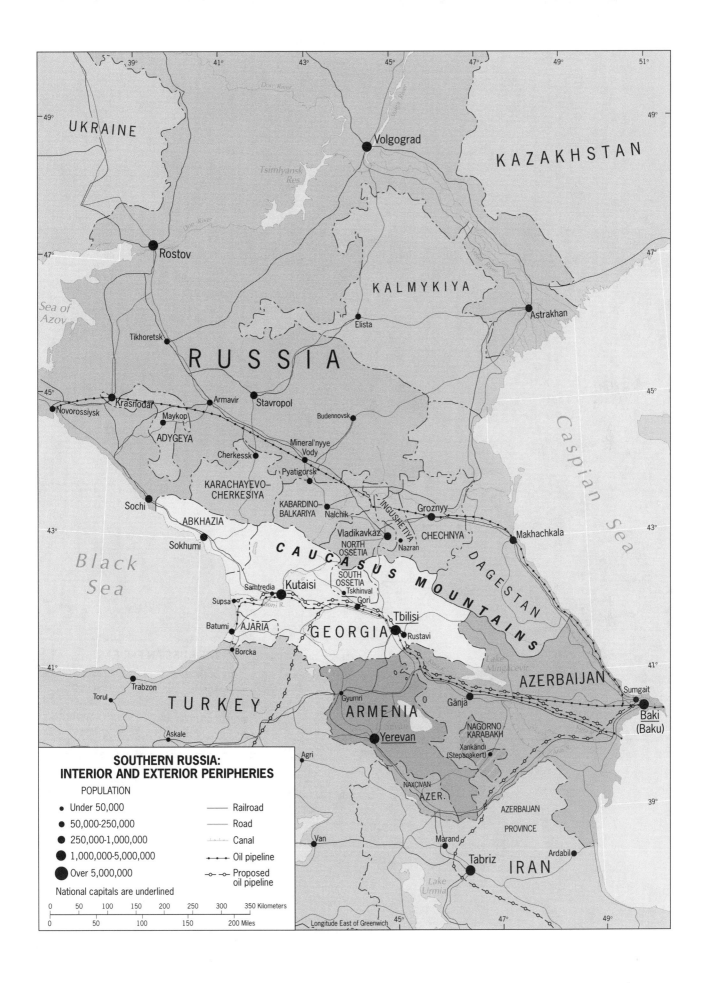

SOUTHERN RUSSIA:
INTERIOR AND EXTERIOR PERIPHERIES

POPULATION

- Under 50,000
- 50,000–250,000
- 250,000–1,000,000
- 1,000,000–5,000,000
- Over 5,000,000

National capitals are underlined

—— Railroad
—— Road
···|··· Canal
•–•–• Oil pipeline
o–o–o Proposed oil pipeline

0 50 100 150 200 250 300 350 Kilometers
0   50   100   150   200 Miles

Longitude East of Greenwich

FIGURE 2-13

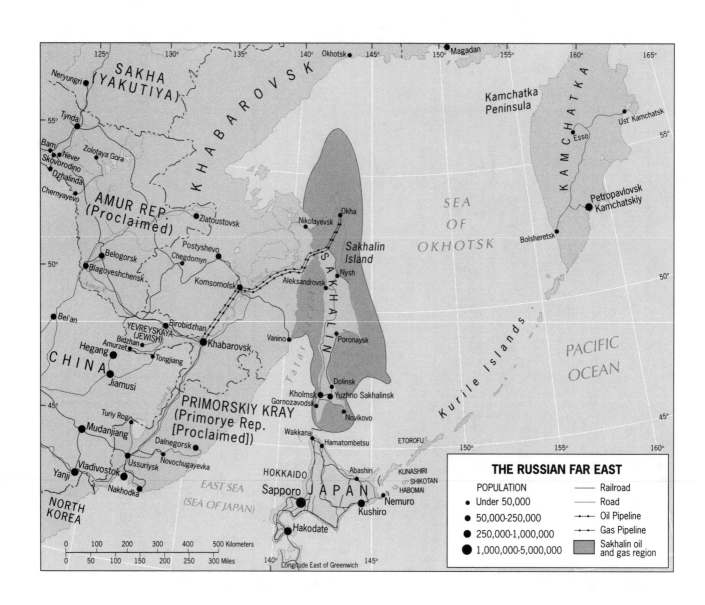

THE RUSSIAN FAR EAST

POPULATION
- Under 50,000
- 50,000–250,000
- 250,000–1,000,000
- 1,000,000–5,000,000

Railroad
Road
Oil Pipeline
Gas Pipeline
Sakhalin oil and gas region

FIGURE 2-14

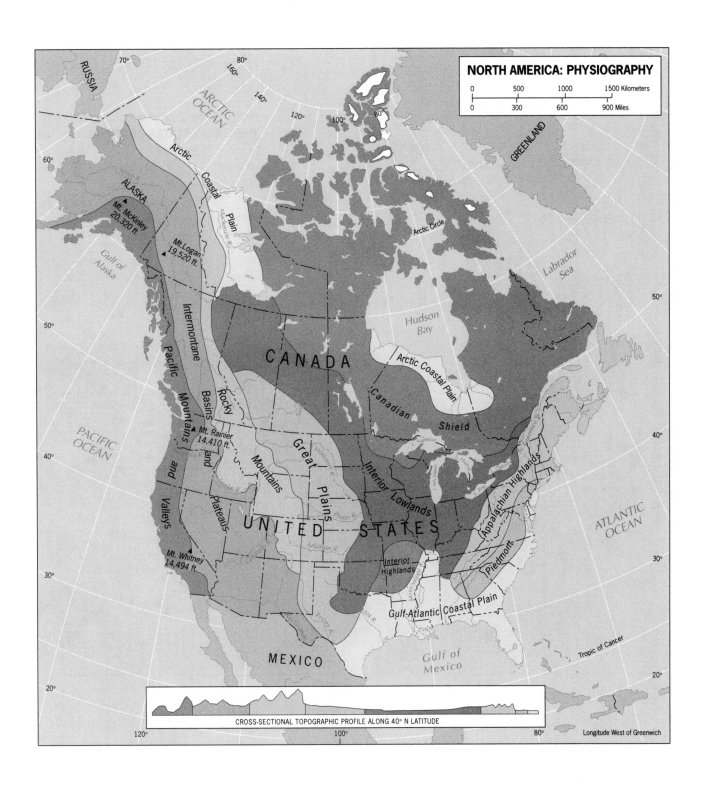

NORTH AMERICA: PHYSIOGRAPHY

0   500   1000   1500 Kilometers

0   300   600   900 Miles

RUSSIA

70°   80°   160°   140°   120°   100°   80°

ARCTIC OCEAN

Arctic   Coastal

60°   ALASKA

Mt. McKinley
20,320 ft.

Mt. Logan
19,520 ft.

Gulf of Alaska

Plain

Mackenzie R.

GREENLAND

Arctic Circle

Labrador Sea

50°

Hudson Bay

CANADA

Arctic Coastal Plain

Canadian

Shield

PACIFIC OCEAN

Intermontane

Pacific   Mountains

Rocky   Basins   Mountains

and

Plateaus   Great   Plains

Mt. Rainier
14,410 ft.

Valleys

Platte R.

Interior   Lowlands

Appalachian Highlands

40°

ATLANTIC OCEAN

Mt. Whitney
14,494 ft.

Arkansas R.

Interior
Highlands

Piedmont

30°

MEXICO

Gulf-Atlantic Coastal Plain

Mississippi R.

Gulf of Mexico

Tropic of Cancer

20°

120°   100°   80°

CROSS-SECTIONAL TOPOGRAPHIC PROFILE ALONG 40° N LATITUDE

Longitude West of Greenwich

       FIGURE 3-2

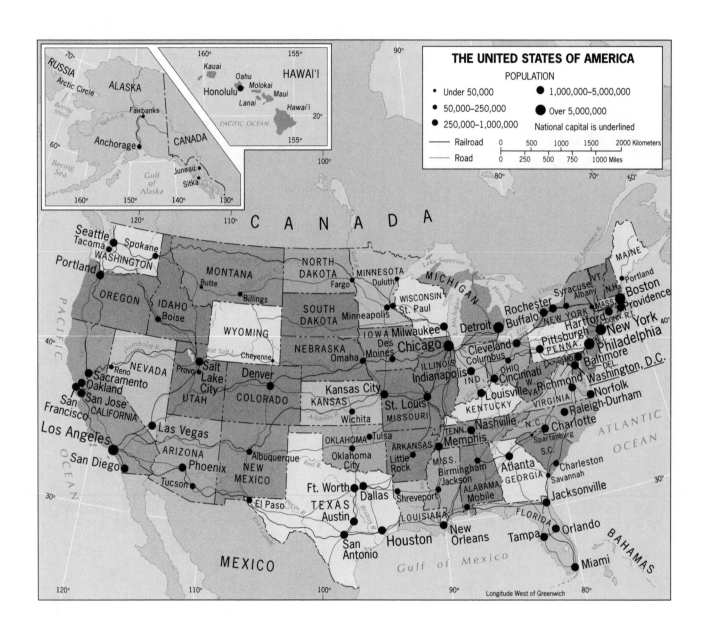

FIGURE 3-3

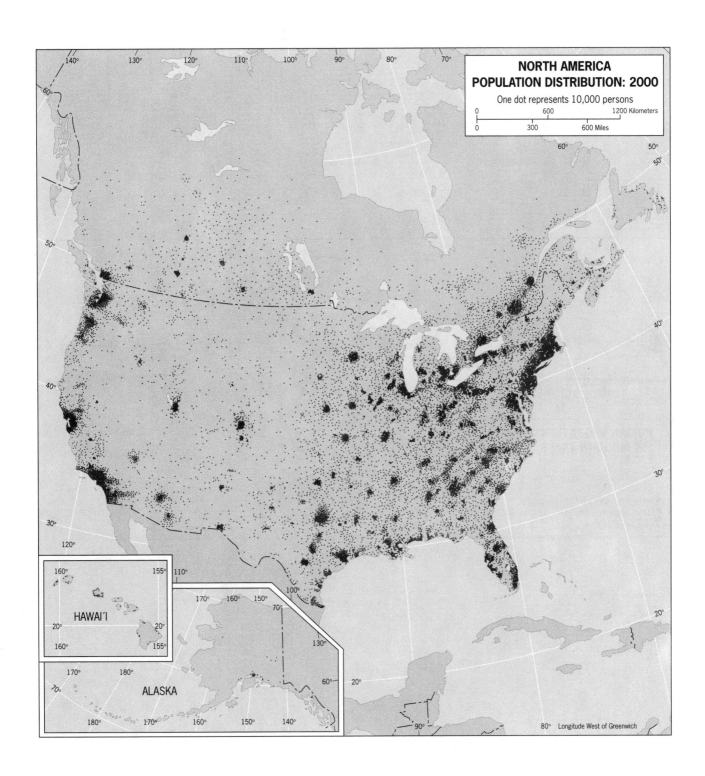

**NORTH AMERICA
POPULATION DISTRIBUTION: 2000**

One dot represents 10,000 persons

HAWAI'I

ALASKA

59

FIGURE 3-4

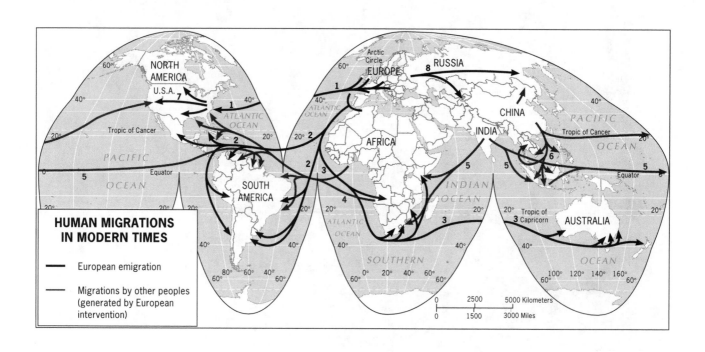

HUMAN MIGRATIONS IN MODERN TIMES

— European emigration

— Migrations by other peoples (generated by European intervention)

FIGURE 3-5

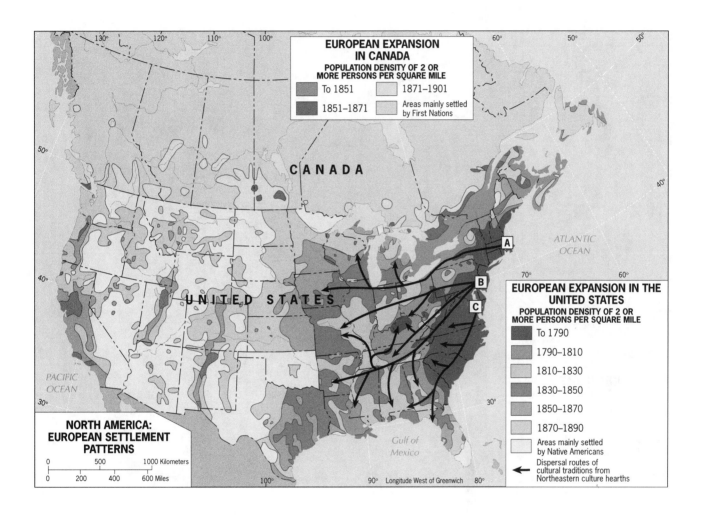

NORTH AMERICA: EUROPEAN SETTLEMENT PATTERNS

EUROPEAN EXPANSION IN CANADA
POPULATION DENSITY OF 2 OR MORE PERSONS PER SQUARE MILE
- To 1851
- 1851–1871
- 1871–1901
- Areas mainly settled by First Nations

EUROPEAN EXPANSION IN THE UNITED STATES
POPULATION DENSITY OF 2 OR MORE PERSONS PER SQUARE MILE
- To 1790
- 1790–1810
- 1810–1830
- 1830–1850
- 1850–1870
- 1870–1890
- Areas mainly settled by Native Americans
- Dispersal routes of cultural traditions from Northeastern culture hearths

FIGURE 3-6

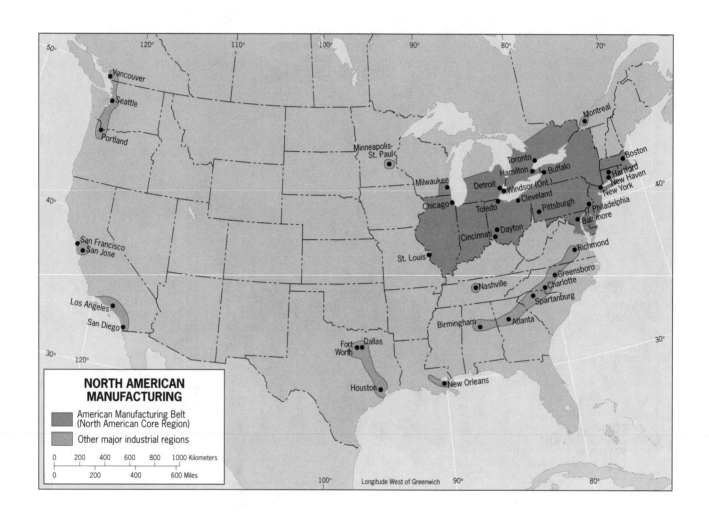

NORTH AMERICAN MANUFACTURING

■ American Manufacturing Belt (North American Core Region)

■ Other major industrial regions

0　200　400　600　800　1000 Kilometers
0　　200　　400　　600 Miles

Longitude West of Greenwich

62

FIGURE 3-7

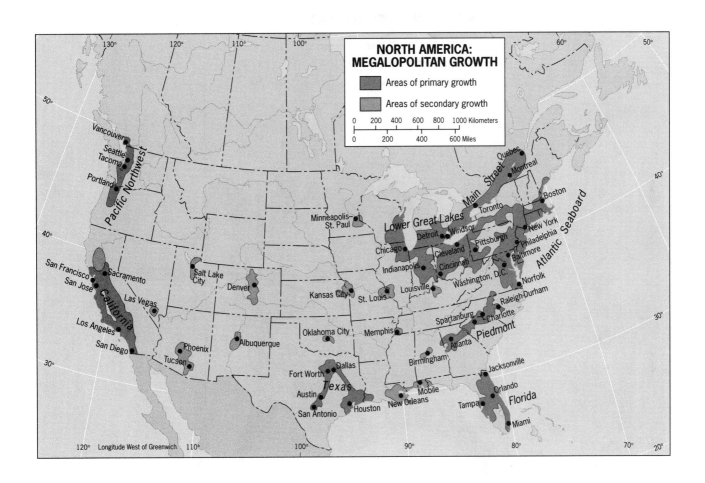

NORTH AMERICA: MEGALOPOLITAN GROWTH

Areas of primary growth

Areas of secondary growth

0   200   400   600   800   1000 Kilometers

0   200   400   600 Miles

63

FIGURE 3-8

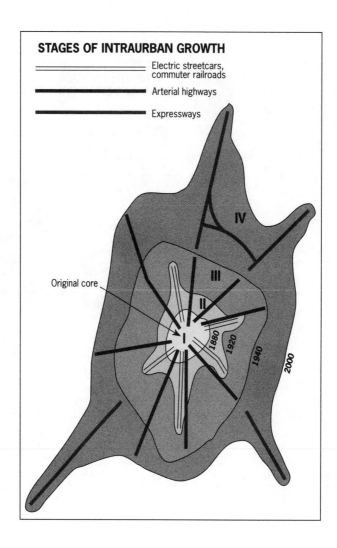

STAGES OF INTRAURBAN GROWTH

Electric streetcars, commuter railroads
Arterial highways
Expressways

Original core

I
II
III
IV

1880
1920
1940
2000

FIGURE 3-9

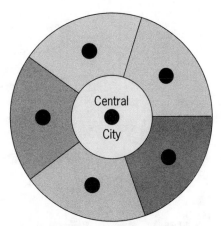

**IDEAL FORM OF MULTICENTERED
URBAN REALMS MODEL**

FIGURE 3-10

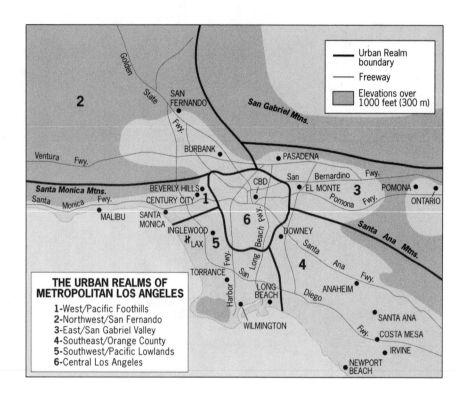

THE URBAN REALMS OF METROPOLITAN LOS ANGELES

1-West/Pacific Foothills
2-Northwest/San Fernando
3-East/San Gabriel Valley
4-Southeast/Orange County
5-Southwest/Pacific Lowlands
6-Central Los Angeles

FIGURE 3-11

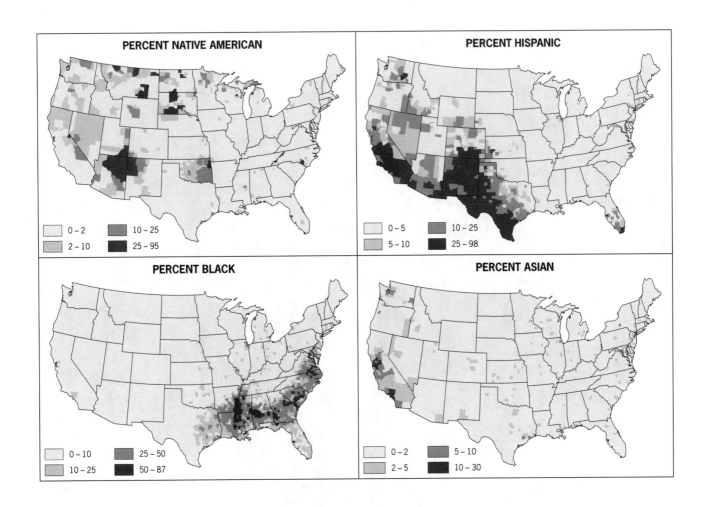

PERCENT NATIVE AMERICAN

| | 0 – 2 | | 10 – 25 |
| | 2 – 10 | | 25 – 95 |

PERCENT HISPANIC

| | 0 – 5 | | 10 – 25 |
| | 5 – 10 | | 25 – 98 |

PERCENT BLACK

| | 0 – 10 | | 25 – 50 |
| | 10 – 25 | | 50 – 87 |

PERCENT ASIAN

| | 0 – 2 | | 5 – 10 |
| | 2 – 5 | | 10 – 30 |

FIGURE 3-12

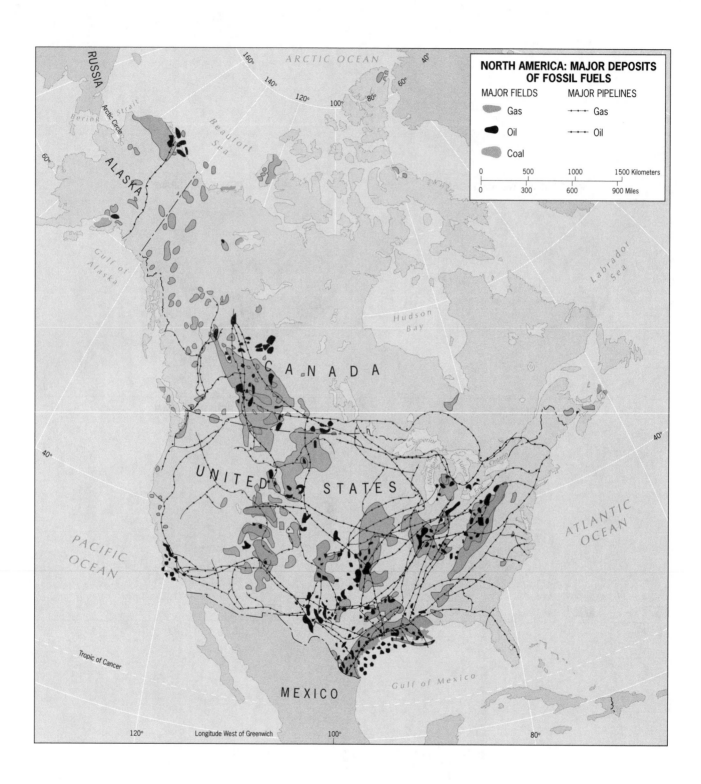

FIGURE 3-13

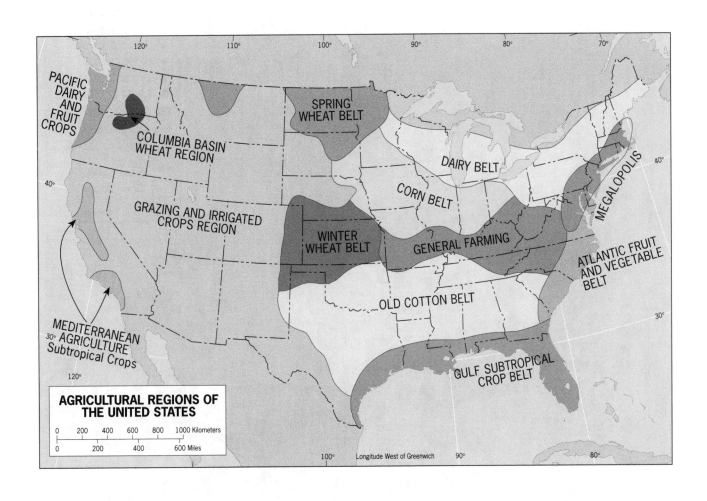

AGRICULTURAL REGIONS OF THE UNITED STATES

PACIFIC DAIRY AND FRUIT CROPS

COLUMBIA BASIN WHEAT REGION

SPRING WHEAT BELT

DAIRY BELT

GRAZING AND IRRIGATED CROPS REGION

CORN BELT

MEGALOPOLIS

WINTER WHEAT BELT

GENERAL FARMING

ATLANTIC FRUIT AND VEGETABLE BELT

MEDITERRANEAN AGRICULTURE Subtropical Crops

OLD COTTON BELT

GULF SUBTROPICAL CROP BELT

0   200   400   600   800   1000 Kilometers
0   200   400   600 Miles

Longitude West of Greenwich

FIGURE 3-14

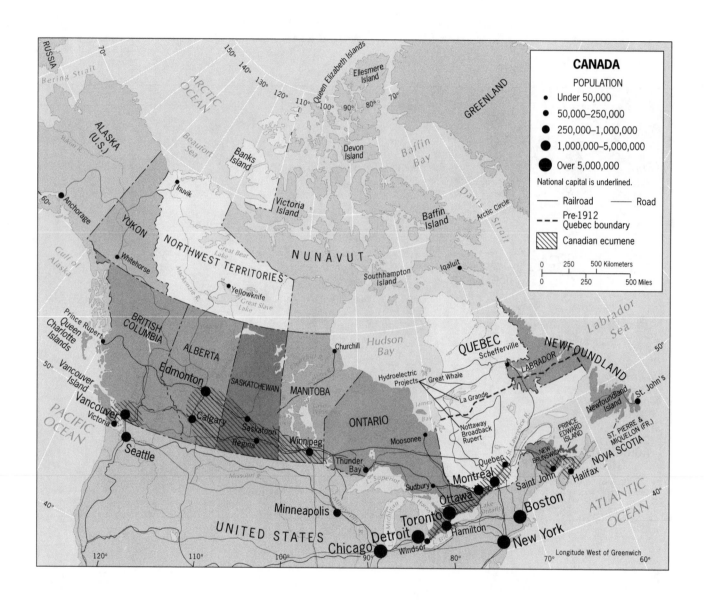

70

FIGURE 3-15

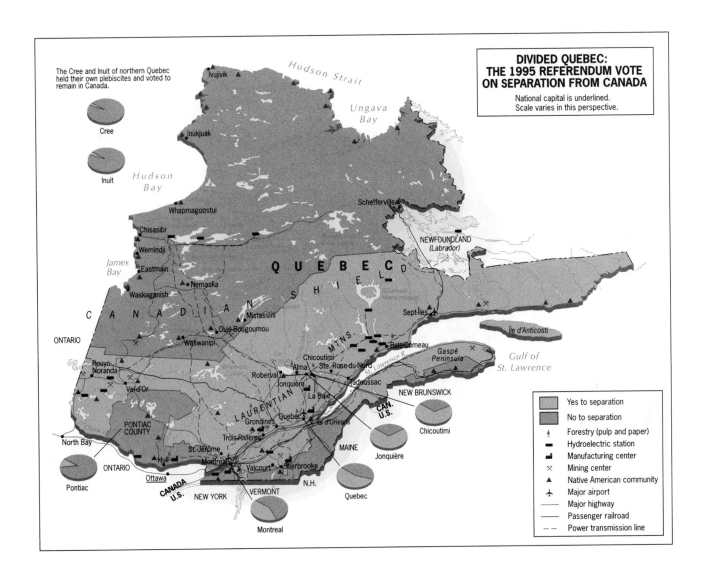

DIVIDED QUEBEC: THE 1995 REFERENDUM VOTE ON SEPARATION FROM CANADA

National capital is underlined.
Scale varies in this perspective.

The Cree and Inuit of northern Quebec held their own plebiscites and voted to remain in Canada.

Cree

Inuit

Hudson Strait

Ungava Bay

Hudson Bay

Ivujivik

Inukjuak

Whapmagoostui

Chisasibi

Wemindji

Eastmain

James Bay

Nemaska

Waskaganish

Schefferville

NEWFOUNDLAND (Labrador)

QUEBEC SHIELD

CANADIAN

ONTARIO

Mistassini

Oujé-Bougoumou

Waswanipi

Reservoir Manicouagan

Sept-Îles

Île d'Anticosti

Rouyn-Noranda

Val-d'Or

Reservoir Gouin

Chicoutimi

Roberval

Alma

Ste-Rose-du-Nord

Baie-Comeau

Gaspé Peninsula

Gulf of St. Lawrence

MTNS.

St. Lawrence R.

Tadoussac

Jonquière

La Baie

NEW BRUNSWICK

Chicoutimi

PONTIAC COUNTY

North Bay

ONTARIO

Pontiac

Hull

Ottawa

CANADA U.S.

NEW YORK

St-Jérôme

Montreal

Valcourt

VERMONT

Montreal

LAURENTIAN

Grondines

Québec

Trois-Rivières

Île d'Orléans

Sherbrooke

N.H.

MAINE

CAN. U.S.

Jonquière

Quebec

Legend:
- Yes to separation
- No to separation
- Forestry (pulp and paper)
- Hydroelectric station
- Manufacturing center
- Mining center
- Native American community
- Major airport
- Major highway
- Passenger railroad
- Power transmission line

71

FIGURE 3-16

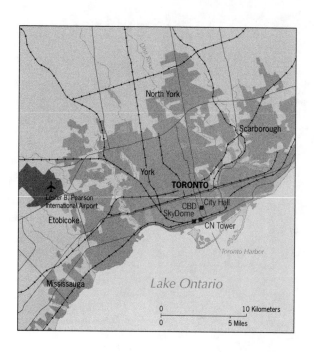

TORONTO

REGIONS OF THE NORTH AMERICAN REALM

FIGURE 3-17

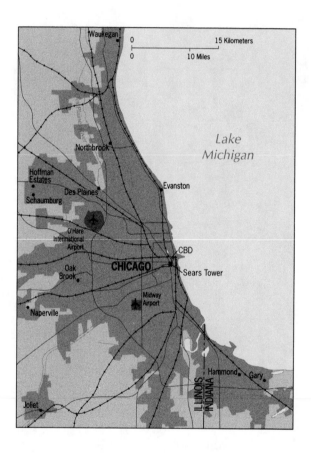

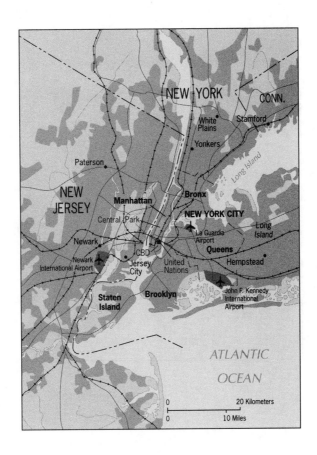

NEW YORK

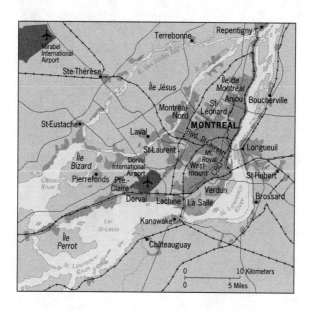

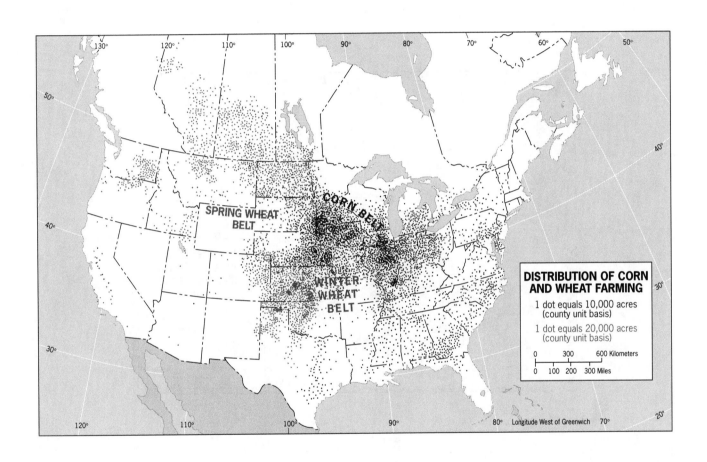

DISTRIBUTION OF CORN AND WHEAT FARMING

1 dot equals 10,000 acres (county unit basis)

1 dot equals 20,000 acres (county unit basis)

FIGURE 3-18

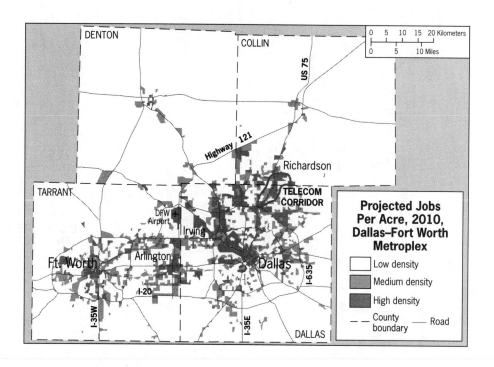

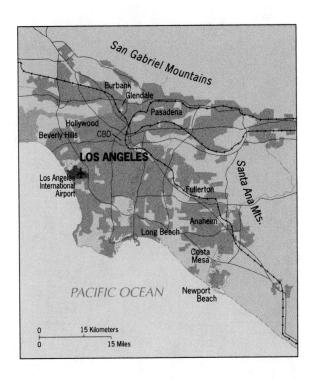

79

LOS ANGELES

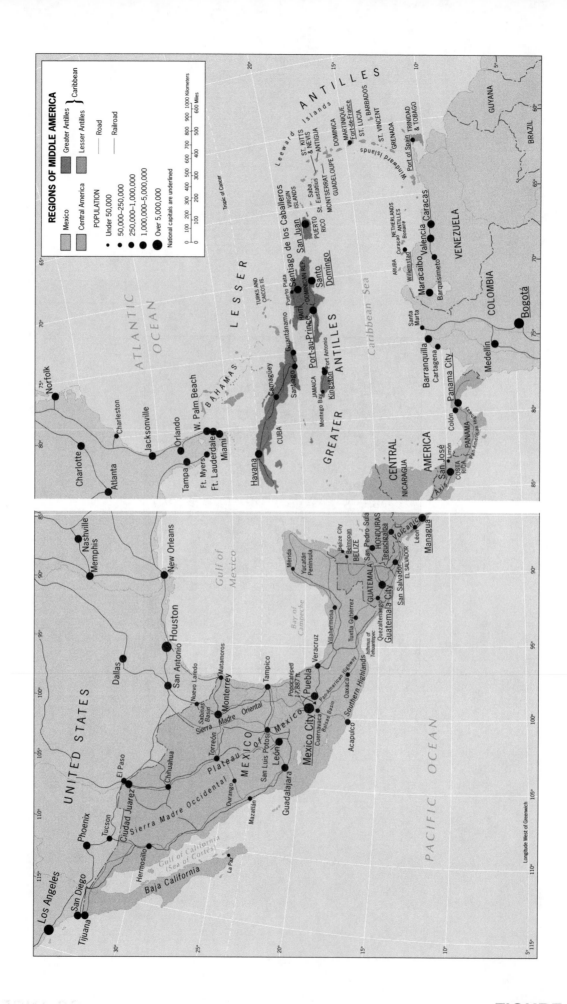

80

FIGURE 4-2

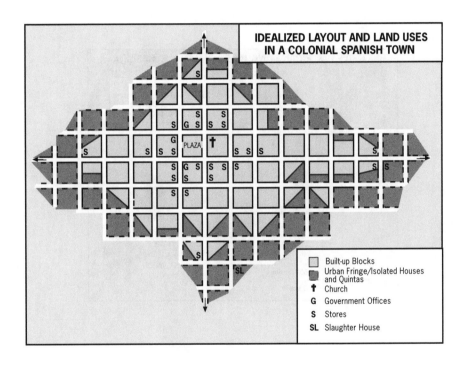

IDEALIZED LAYOUT AND LAND USES
IN A COLONIAL SPANISH TOWN

PLAZA

Built-up Blocks
Urban Fringe/Isolated Houses and Quintas
† Church
G Government Offices
S Stores
SL Slaughter House

81

FIGURE 4-3

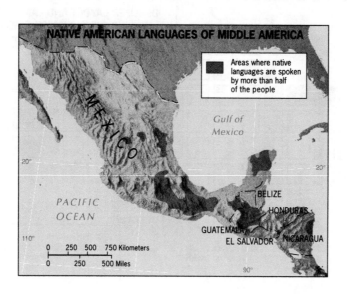

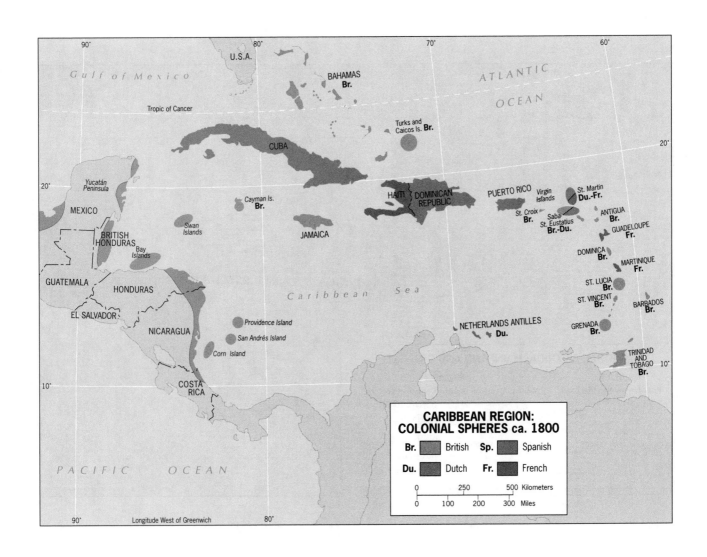

CARIBBEAN REGION: COLONIAL SPHERES ca. 1800

Br.	British	**Sp.**	Spanish
Du.	Dutch	**Fr.**	French

Kilometers: 0 — 250 — 500
Miles: 0 — 100 — 200 — 300

FIGURE 4-5

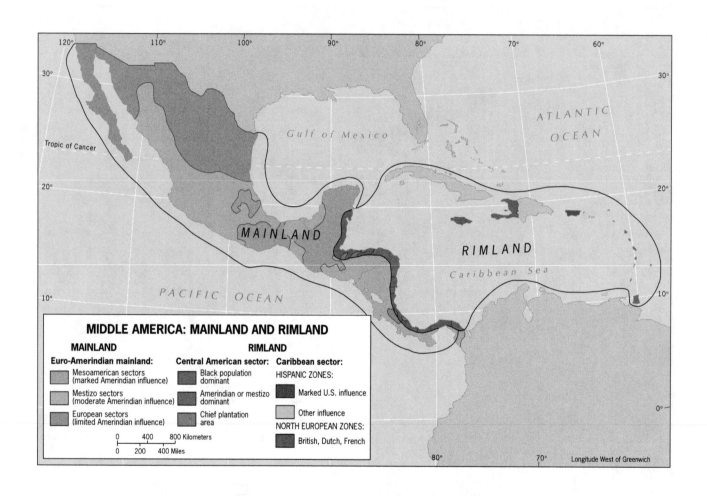

MIDDLE AMERICA: MAINLAND AND RIMLAND

MAINLAND

Euro-Amerindian mainland:

- Mesoamerican sectors (marked Amerindian influence)
- Mestizo sectors (moderate Amerindian influence)
- European sectors (limited Amerindian influence)

0   400   800 Kilometers
0   200   400 Miles

RIMLAND

Central American sector:

- Black population dominant
- Amerindian or mestizo dominant
- Chief plantation area

Caribbean sector:

HISPANIC ZONES:

- Marked U.S. influence
- Other influence

NORTH EUROPEAN ZONES:

- British, Dutch, French

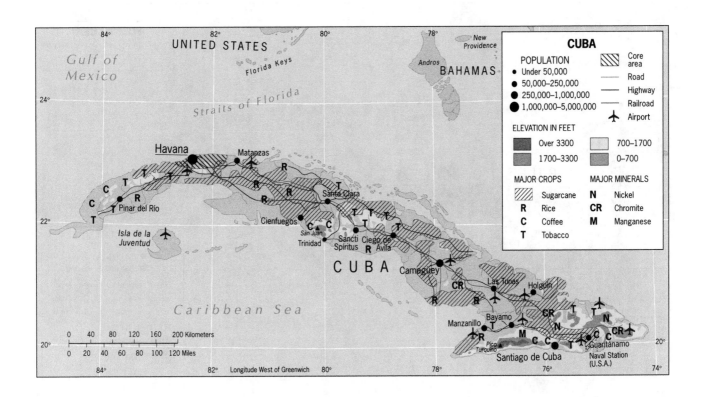

FIGURE 4-7

85

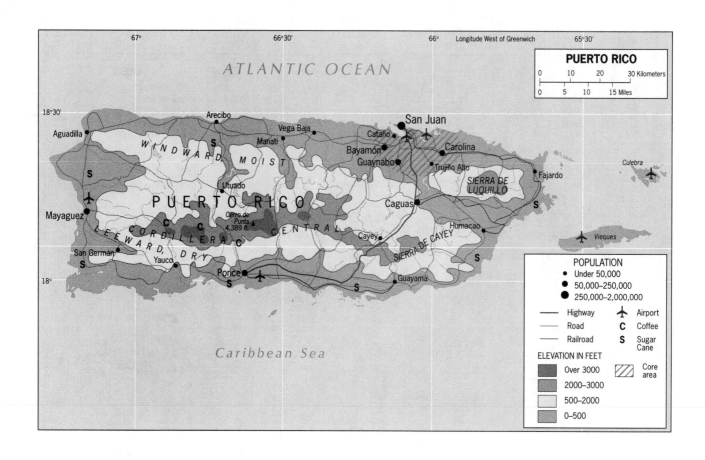

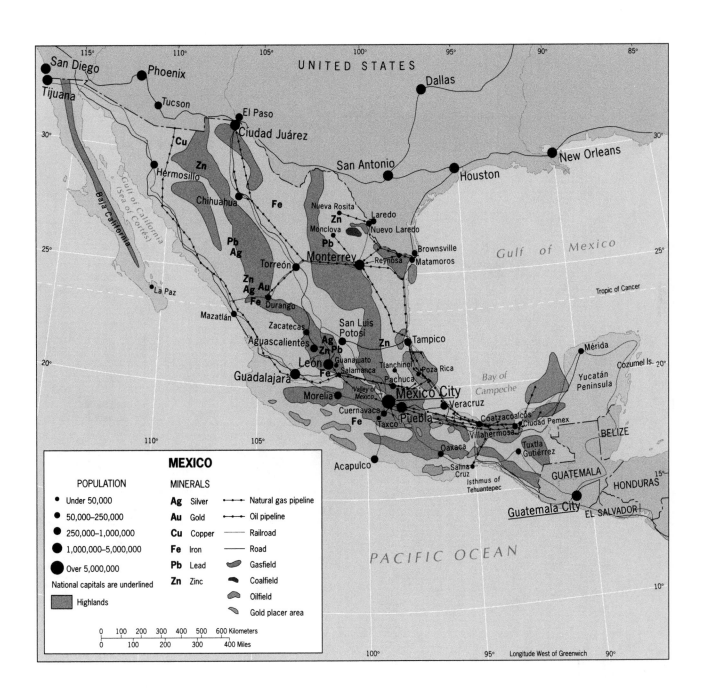

MEXICO

POPULATION

- Under 50,000
- 50,000–250,000
- 250,000–1,000,000
- 1,000,000–5,000,000
- Over 5,000,000

National capitals are underlined

Highlands

MINERALS

Ag Silver
Au Gold
Cu Copper
Fe Iron
Pb Lead
Zn Zinc

Natural gas pipeline
Oil pipeline
Railroad
Road
Gasfield
Coalfield
Oilfield
Gold placer area

0 100 200 300 400 500 600 Kilometers
0 100 200 300 400 Miles

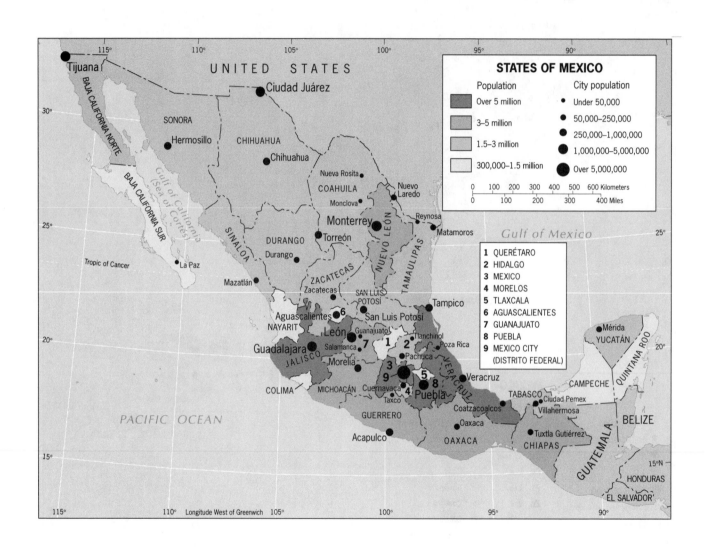

STATES OF MEXICO

Population
- Over 5 million
- 3–5 million
- 1.5–3 million
- 300,000–1.5 million

City population
- Under 50,000
- 50,000–250,000
- 250,000–1,000,000
- 1,000,000–5,000,000
- Over 5,000,000

1 QUERÉTARO
2 HIDALGO
3 MEXICO
4 MORELOS
5 TLAXCALA
6 AGUASCALIENTES
7 GUANAJUATO
8 PUEBLA
9 MEXICO CITY
(DISTRITO FEDERAL)

FIGURE 4-10

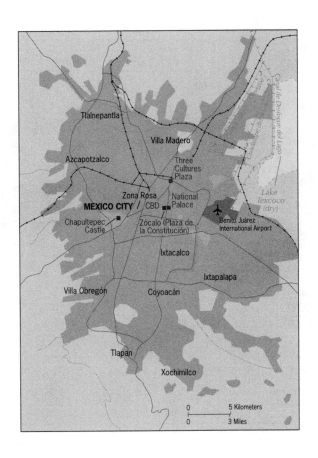

Tlalnepantla

Villa Madero

Azcapotzalco

Three
Cultures
Plaza

Zona Rosa

MEXICO CITY CBD National
Palace

Chapultepec
Castle

Zócalo (Plaza de
la Constitución)

Benito Juárez
International Airport

Lake
Texcoco
(dry)

Canal de Desfogue del Lago

Ixtacalco

Ixtapalapa

Villa Obregón

Coyoacán

Tlalpan

Xochimilco

0   5 Kilometers

0   3 Miles

MEXICO CITY

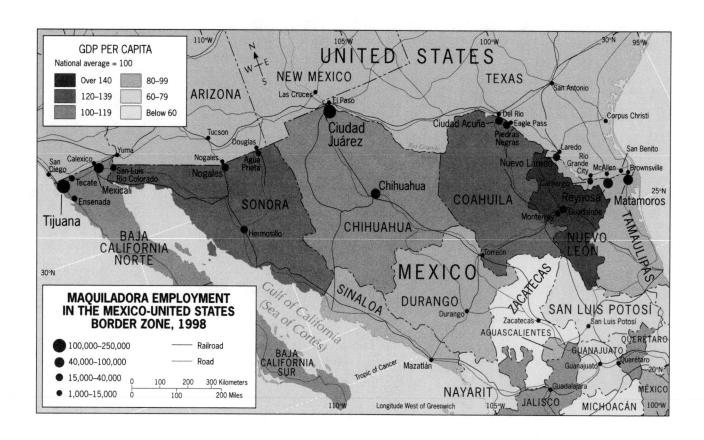

GDP PER CAPITA

National average = 100

- Over 140
- 120–139
- 100–119
- 80–99
- 60–79
- Below 60

MAQUILADORA EMPLOYMENT IN THE MEXICO-UNITED STATES BORDER ZONE, 1998

- 100,000–250,000
- 40,000–100,000
- 15,000–40,000
- 1,000–15,000

—— Railroad
—— Road

0   100   200   300 Kilometers
0   100   200 Miles

FIGURE 4-11

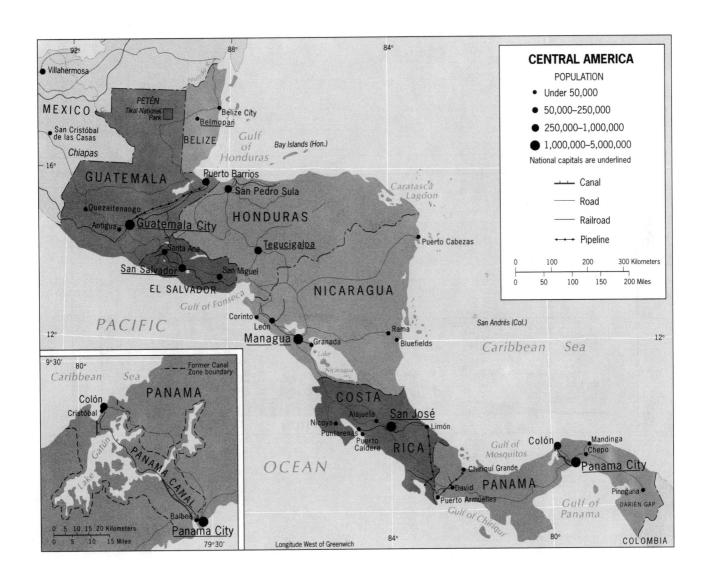

91

FIGURE 4-12

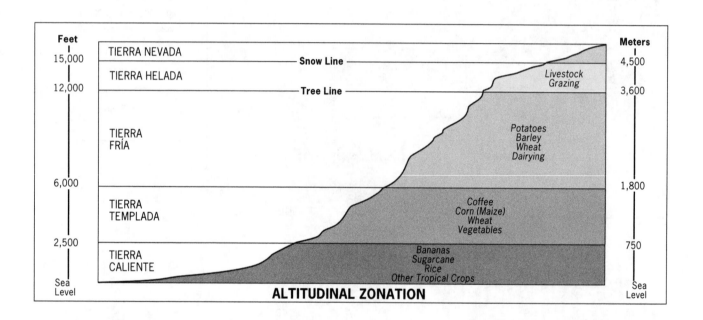

ALTITUDINAL ZONATION

FIGURE 4-13

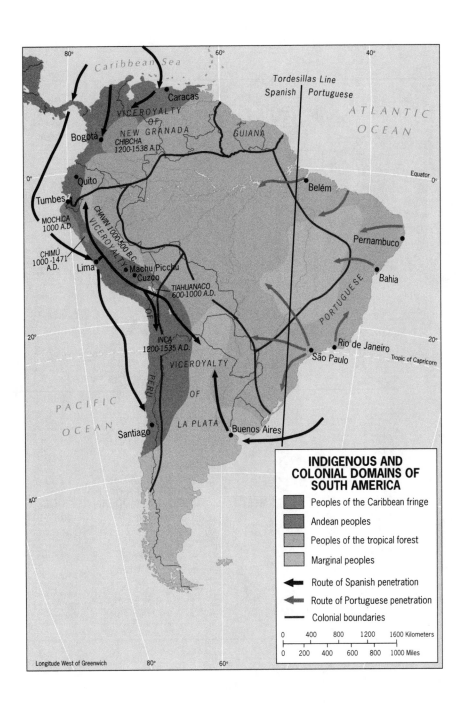

INDIGENOUS AND COLONIAL DOMAINS OF SOUTH AMERICA

- Peoples of the Caribbean fringe
- Andean peoples
- Peoples of the tropical forest
- Marginal peoples
- ← Route of Spanish penetration
- ← Route of Portuguese penetration
- — Colonial boundaries

0   400   800   1200   1600 Kilometers

0   200   400   600   800   1000 Miles

93

FIGURE 5-2

SOUTH AMERICA: POLITICAL UNITS AND MODERN REGIONS

POPULATION
- Under 50,000
- 50,000–250,000
- 250,000–1,000,000
- 1,000,000–5,000,000
- Over 5,000,000

National capitals are underlined

REGIONS
- Brazil
- The North
- The West
- The Southern Cone

0   400   800   1200   1600 Kilometers
0   200   400   600   800   1000 Miles

FIGURE 5-3

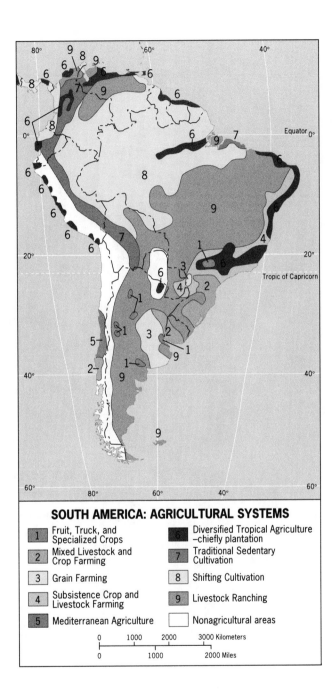

SOUTH AMERICA: AGRICULTURAL SYSTEMS

1 Fruit, Truck, and Specialized Crops

2 Mixed Livestock and Crop Farming

3 Grain Farming

4 Subsistence Crop and Livestock Farming

5 Mediterranean Agriculture

6 Diversified Tropical Agriculture –chiefly plantation

7 Traditional Sedentary Cultivation

8 Shifting Cultivation

9 Livestock Ranching

Nonagricultural areas

0 1000 2000 3000 Kilometers

0 1000 2000 Miles

FIGURE 5-4

SOUTH AMERICA: CULTURE SPHERES

- Tropical-plantation
- European-commercial
- Amerind-subsistence
- Mestizo-transitional
- Undifferentiated

0   400   800   1200 Kilometers
0   200   400   600 Miles

FIGURE 5-5

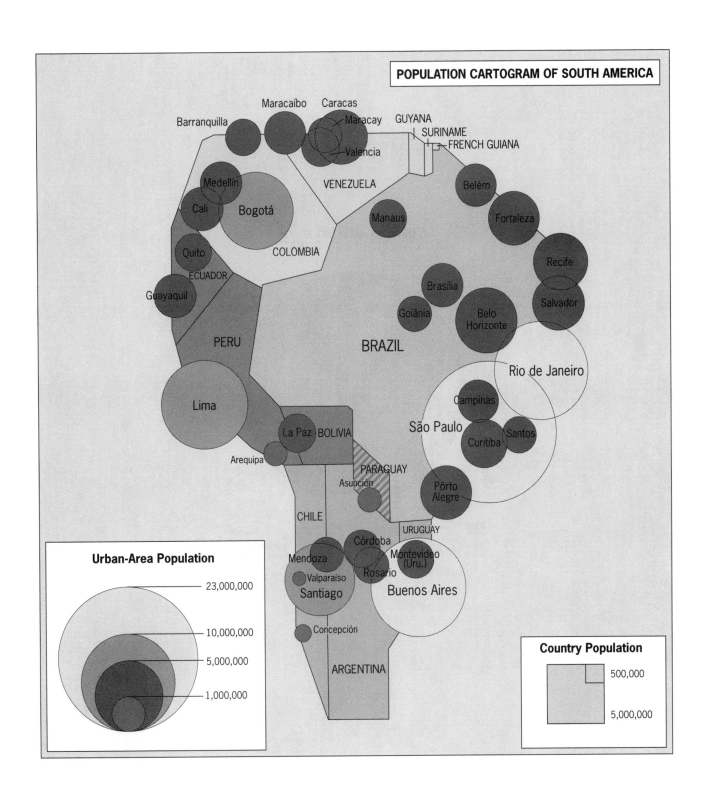

POPULATION CARTOGRAM OF SOUTH AMERICA

Barranquilla
Maracaíbo Caracas
Maracay
GUYANA
SURINAME
FRENCH GUIANA
Valencia
VENEZUELA
Belém
Medellín
Cali
Bogotá
Fortaleza
Manaus
Quito
COLOMBIA
ECUADOR
Recife
Guayaquil
Brasília
Salvador
Goiânia
Belo
Horizonte
PERU
BRAZIL
Rio de Janeiro
Campinas
Lima
São Paulo
Santos
Curitiba
La Paz BOLIVIA
Arequipa
PARAGUAY
Asunción
Pôrto
Alegre
CHILE
URUGUAY
Córdoba
Montevideo
(Uru.)
Mendoza
Rosario
Valparaíso
Santiago
Buenos Aires
Concepción
ARGENTINA

Urban-Area Population

— 23,000,000

— 10,000,000

— 5,000,000

— 1,000,000

Country Population

500,000

5,000,000

FIGURE 5-6

A GENERALIZED MODEL OF
LATIN AMERICAN CITY STRUCTURE

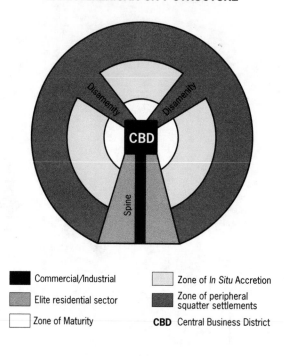

Commercial/Industrial   Zone of *In Situ* Accretion

Elite residential sector   Zone of peripheral
squatter settlements

Zone of Maturity   **CBD** Central Business District

98

FIGURE 5-7

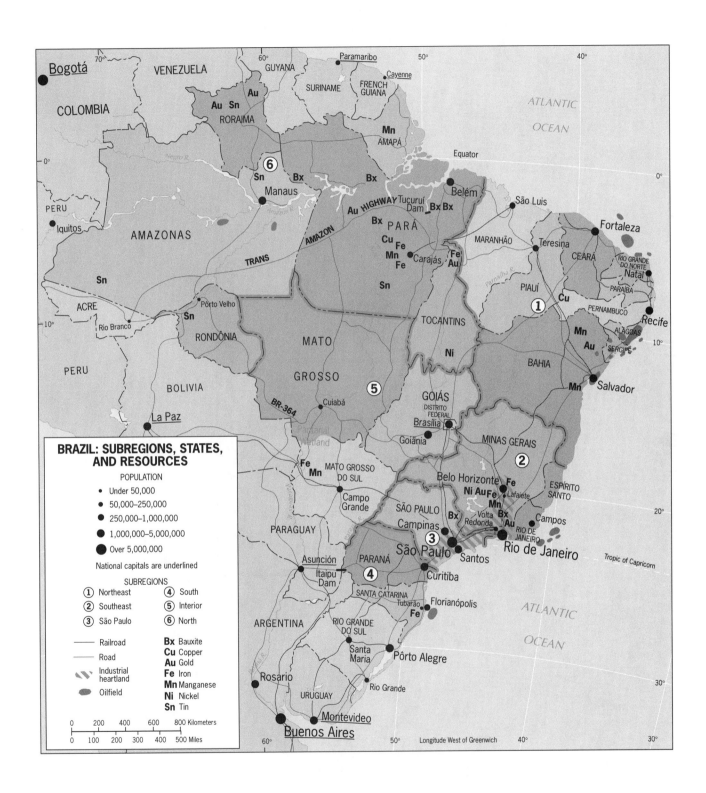

BRAZIL: SUBREGIONS, STATES, AND RESOURCES

POPULATION
- • Under 50,000
- • 50,000–250,000
- • 250,000–1,000,000
- ● 1,000,000–5,000,000
- ● Over 5,000,000

National capitals are underlined

SUBREGIONS
① Northeast   ④ South
② Southeast   ⑤ Interior
③ São Paulo   ⑥ North

— Railroad
— Road

Industrial heartland

Oilfield

Bx Bauxite
Cu Copper
Au Gold
Fe Iron
Mn Manganese
Ni Nickel
Sn Tin

0 200 400 600 800 Kilometers
0 100 200 300 400 500 Miles

FIGURE 5-8

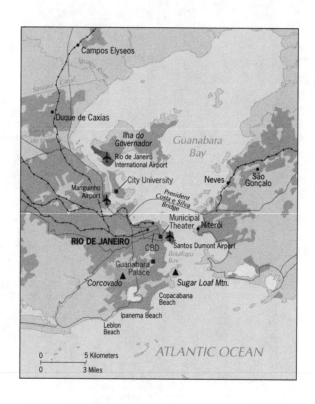

Campos Elyseos

Iguaçu River

Sarapuí Canal

Duque de Caxias

Ilha do Governador

Guanabara Bay

Rio de Janeiro
International Airport

City University

Manguinho
Airport

Neves

São
Gonçalo

President
Costa e Silva
Bridge

Municipal
Theater

Niterói

RIO DE JANEIRO

CBD

Santos Dumont Airport

Botafogo Bay

Guanabara
Palace

Corcovado

Sugar Loaf Mtn.

Copacabana
Beach

Ipanema Beach

Leblon
Beach

ATLANTIC OCEAN

0   5 Kilometers

0   3 Miles

RIO DE JANEIRO

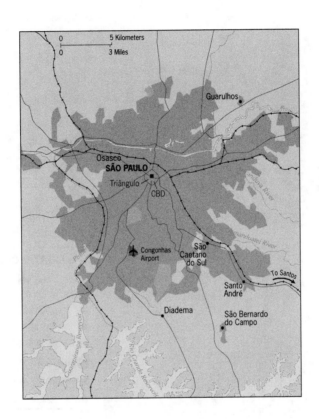

SÃO PAULO

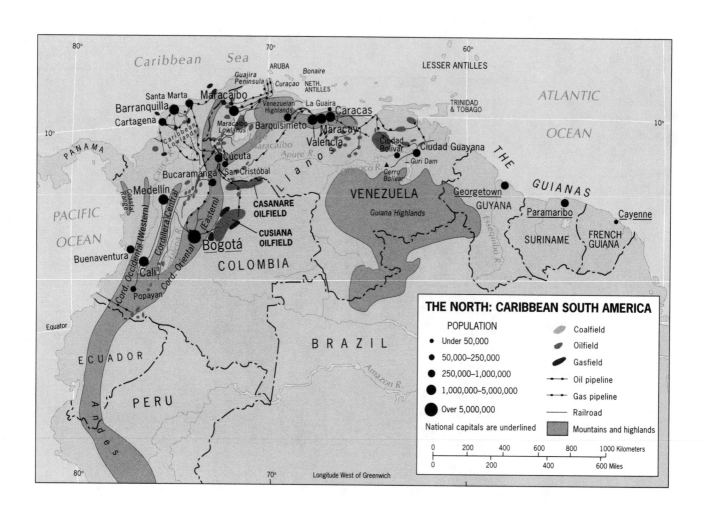

THE NORTH: CARIBBEAN SOUTH AMERICA

POPULATION
- Under 50,000
- 50,000–250,000
- 250,000–1,000,000
- 1,000,000–5,000,000
- Over 5,000,000

National capitals are underlined

Coalfield
Oilfield
Gasfield
Oil pipeline
Gas pipeline
Railroad
Mountains and highlands

| 0 | 200 | 400 | 600 | 800 | 1000 Kilometers |
| 0 | | 200 | | 400 | 600 Miles |

Longitude West of Greenwich

FIGURE 5-9

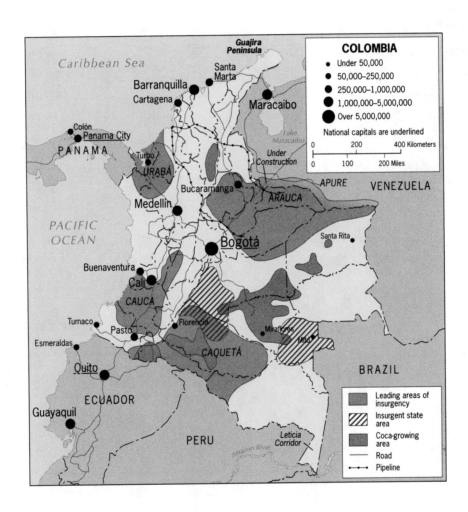

103

FIGURE 5-10

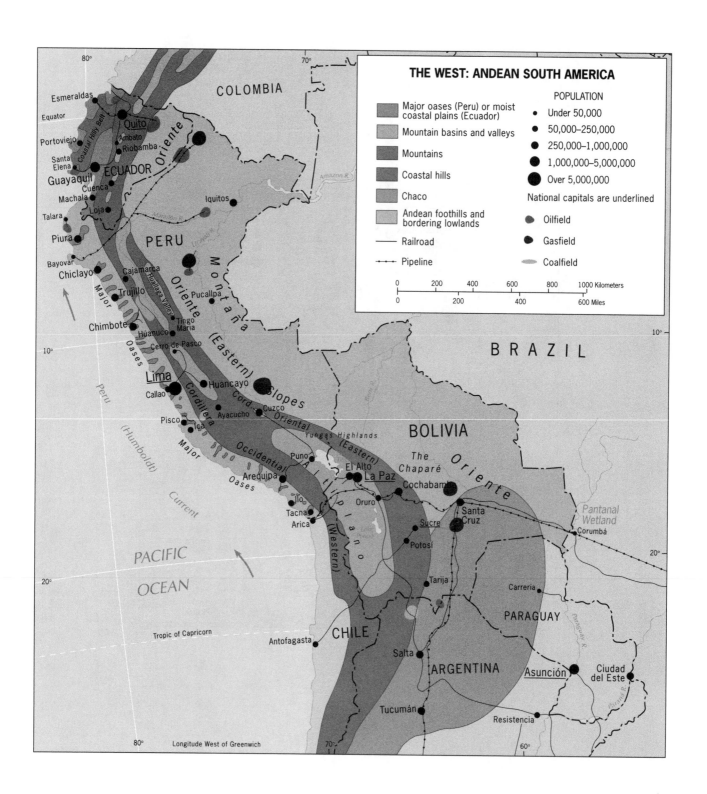

The West: Andean South America

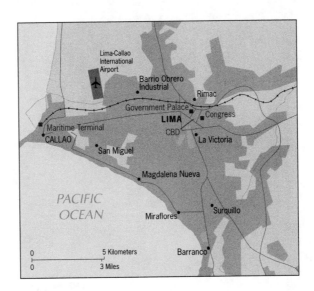

Lima-Callao
International
Airport

Barrio Obrero
Industrial

Rimac

Government Palace

LIMA

Congress

CBD

Maritime Terminal

La Victoria

CALLAO

San Miguel

Magdalena Nueva

PACIFIC
OCEAN

Surquillo

Miraflores

Barranco

0   5 Kilometers
0   3 Miles

LIMA

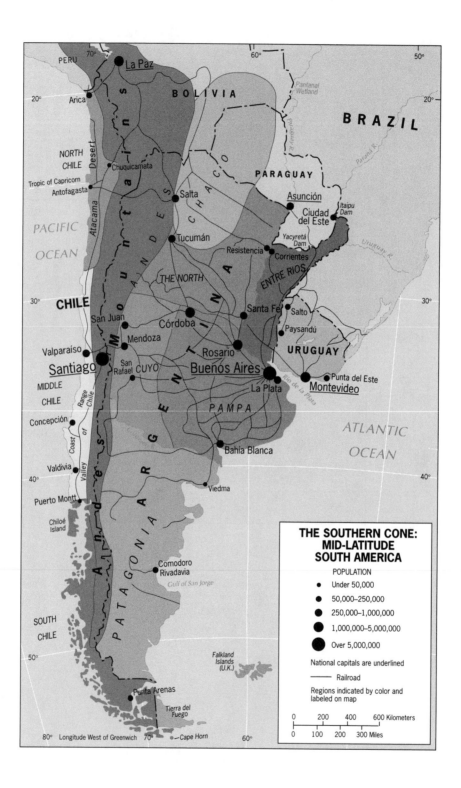

THE SOUTHERN CONE:
MID-LATITUDE
SOUTH AMERICA

POPULATION
• Under 50,000
• 50,000–250,000
● 250,000–1,000,000
● 1,000,000–5,000,000
● Over 5,000,000

National capitals are underlined

— Railroad

Regions indicated by color and labeled on map

0   200   400   600 Kilometers
0 100 200 300 Miles

FIGURE 5-12

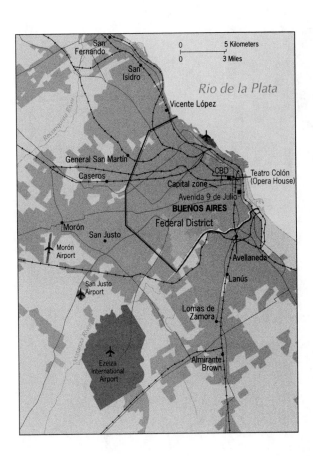

BUENOS AIRES

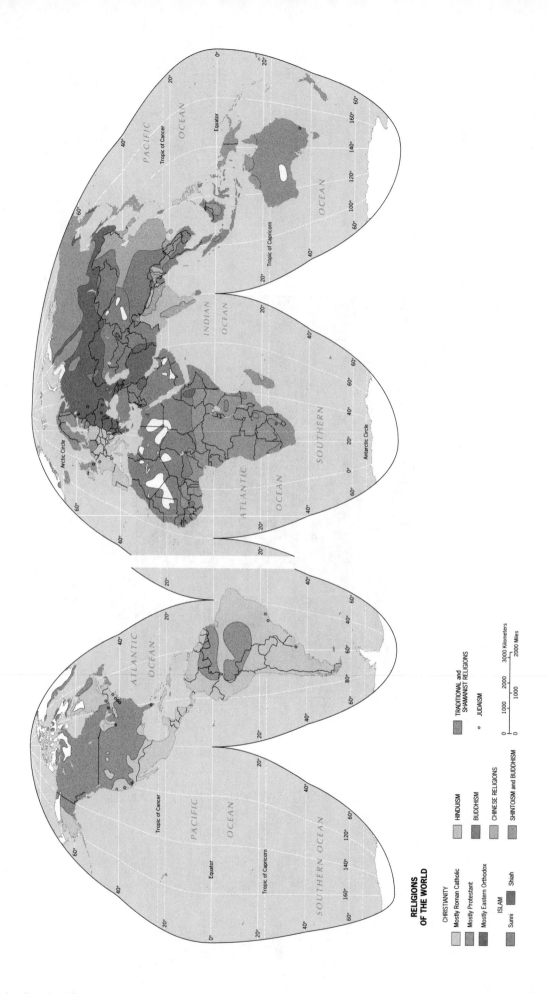

RELIGIONS OF THE WORLD

CHRISTIANITY
- Mostly Roman Catholic
- Mostly Protestant
- Mostly Eastern Orthodox

ISLAM
- Sunni
- Shiah

HINDUISM

BUDDHISM

CHINESE RELIGIONS

SHINTOISM and BUDDHISM

TRADITIONAL and SHAMANIST RELIGIONS

o JUDAISM

0   1000   2000   3000 Kilometers
0   1000   2000 Miles

108

FIGURE 6-2

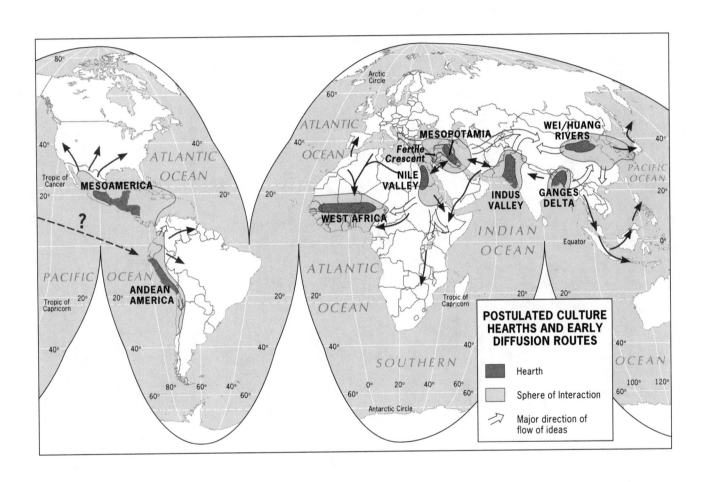

FIGURE 6-3

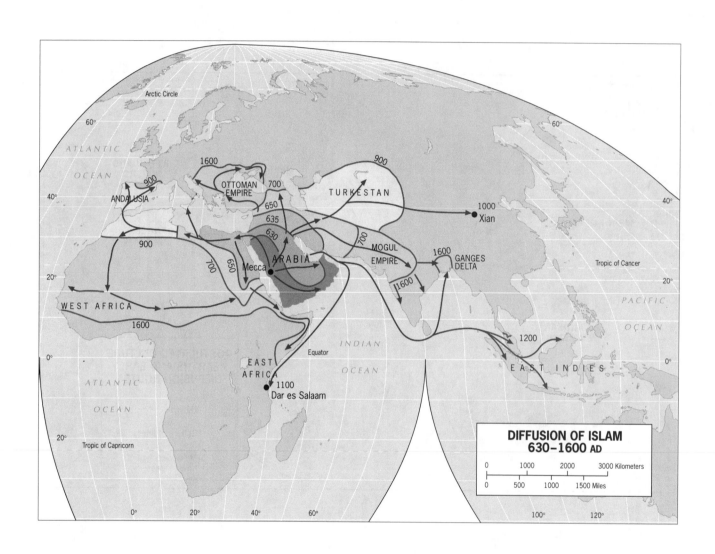

DIFFUSION OF ISLAM
630–1600 AD

| 0 | 1000 | 2000 | 3000 Kilometers |

| 0 | 500 | 1000 | 1500 Miles |

ATLANTIC OCEAN

Arctic Circle

ANDALUSIA

OTTOMAN EMPIRE

TURKESTAN

1600

900

700

900

650

635

630

ARABIA

Mecca

WEST AFRICA

900

700

650

1600

MOGUL EMPIRE

1000
Xian

Tropic of Cancer

1600

GANGES DELTA

1600

PACIFIC OCEAN

INDIAN OCEAN

Equator

EAST AFRICA

1100
Dar es Salaam

1200

EAST INDIES

ATLANTIC OCEAN

Tropic of Capricorn

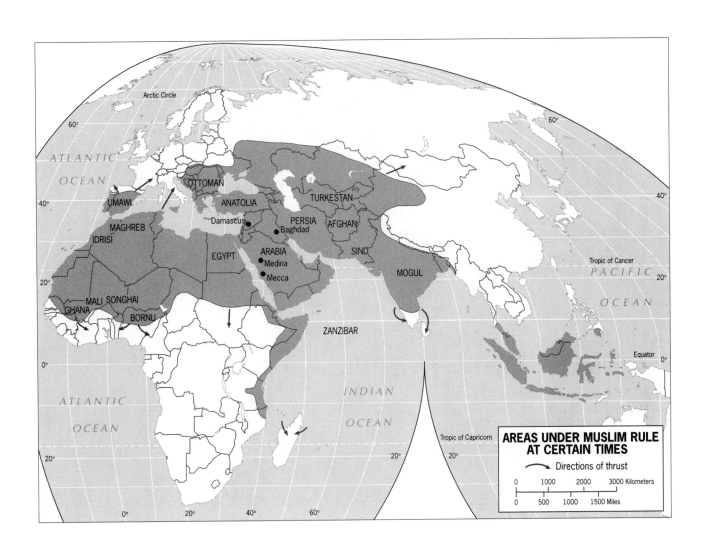

AREAS UNDER MUSLIM RULE AT CERTAIN TIMES

Directions of thrust

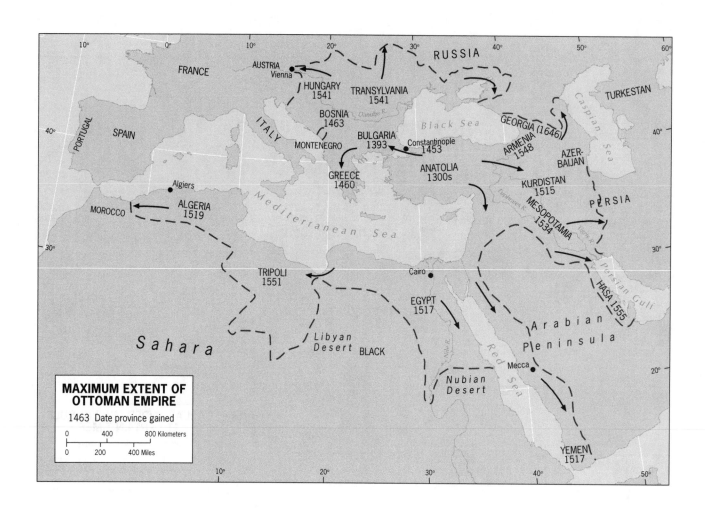

FIGURE 6-6

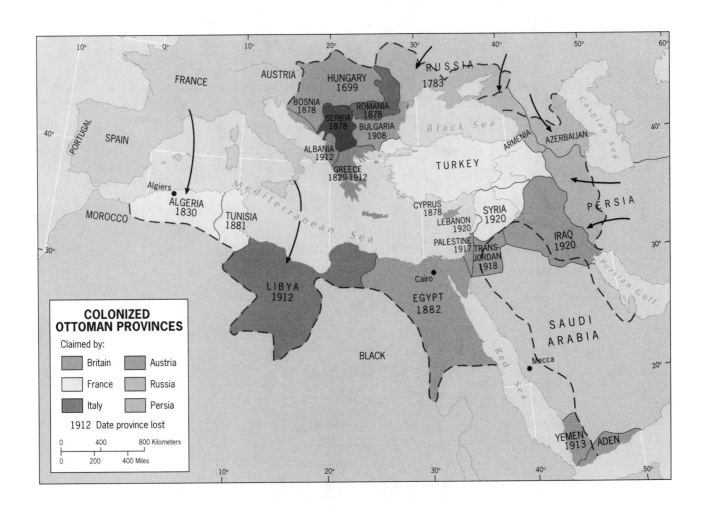

COLONIZED OTTOMAN PROVINCES

Claimed by:

- Britain
- France
- Italy
- Austria
- Russia
- Persia

1912 Date province lost

0   400   800 Kilometers
0 200   400 Miles

FIGURE 6-7

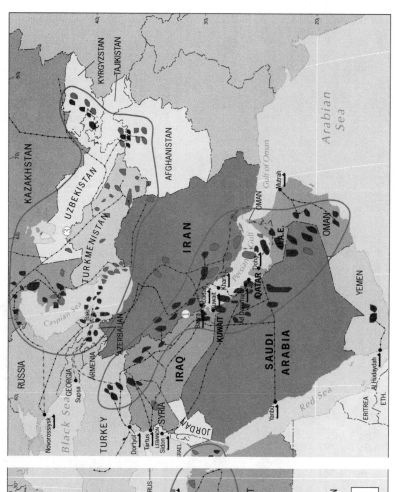

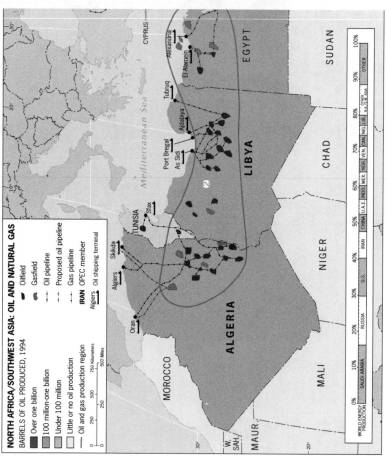

NORTH AFRICA/SOUTHWEST ASIA: OIL AND NATURAL GAS

BARRELS OF OIL PRODUCED, 1994

- Over one billion
- 100 million–one billion
- Under 100 million
- Little or no oil production
- Oil and gas production region

- Oilfield
- Gasfield
- Oil pipeline
- Proposed oil pipeline
- Gas pipeline
- **IRAN** OPEC member
- Algiers Oil shipping terminal

114

FIGURE 6-8

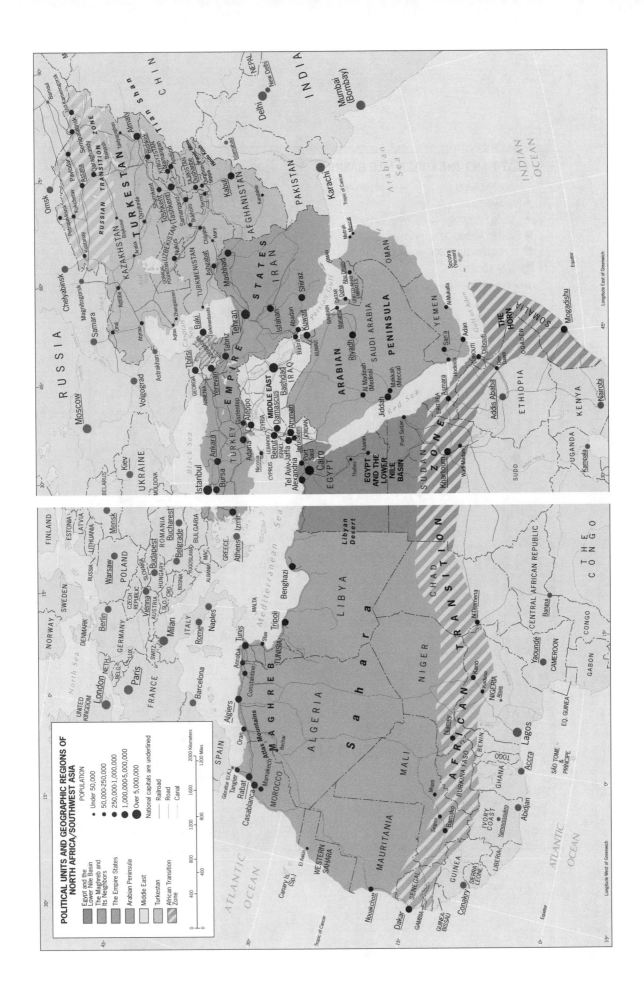

POLITICAL UNITS AND GEOGRAPHIC REGIONS OF
NORTH AFRICA/SOUTHWEST ASIA

Egypt and the
Lower Nile Basin

The Maghreb and
Its Neighbors

The Empire States

Arabian Peninsula

Middle East

Turkestan

African Transition
Zone

POPULATION
· Under 50,000
● 50,000–250,000
● 250,000–1,000,000
● 1,000,000–5,000,000
● Over 5,000,000

National capitals are underlined

—— Railroad
—— Road
—— Canal

0   400   800   1200   1600   2000 Kilometers
0   400   800   1200 Miles

115

FIGURE 6-9

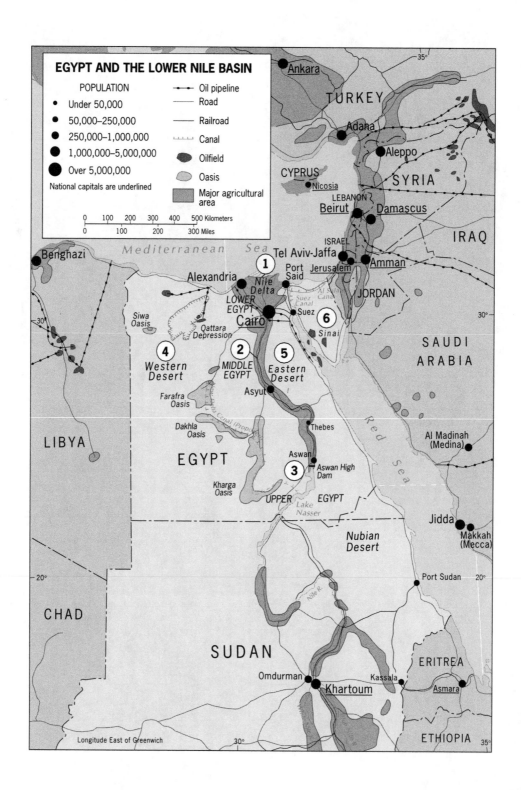

EGYPT AND THE LOWER NILE BASIN

POPULATION
- Under 50,000
- 50,000–250,000
- 250,000–1,000,000
- 1,000,000–5,000,000
- Over 5,000,000

National capitals are underlined

- Oil pipeline
- Road
- Railroad
- Canal
- Oilfield
- Oasis
- Major agricultural area

0   100   200   300   400   500 Kilometers
0   100   200   300 Miles

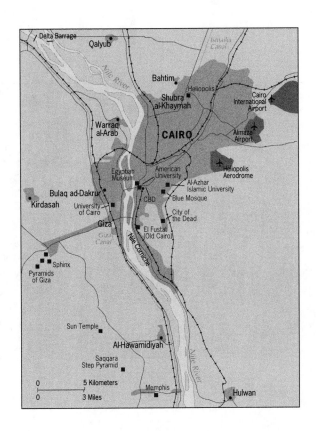

CAIRO

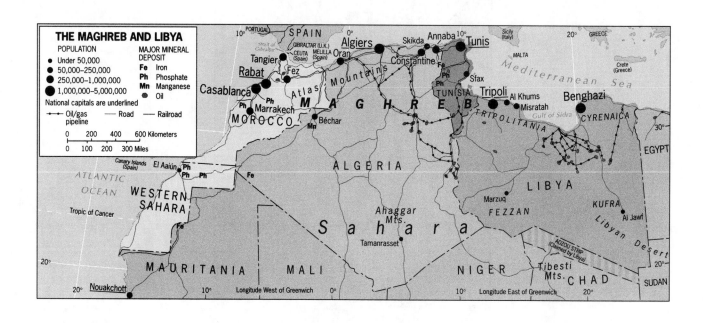

FIGURE 6-11

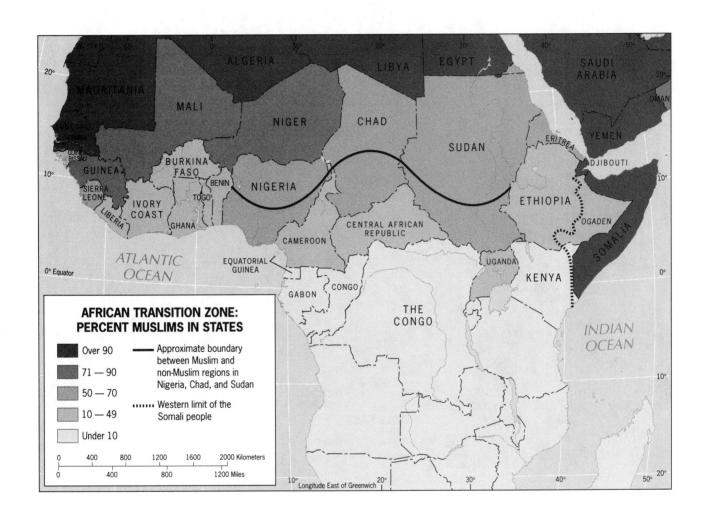

AFRICAN TRANSITION ZONE: PERCENT MUSLIMS IN STATES

- Over 90
- 71 — 90
- 50 — 70
- 10 — 49
- Under 10

— Approximate boundary between Muslim and non-Muslim regions in Nigeria, Chad, and Sudan

······ Western limit of the Somali people

| 0 | 400 | 800 | 1200 | 1600 | 2000 Kilometers |
| 0 | 400 | 800 | 1200 Miles |

FIGURE 6-12

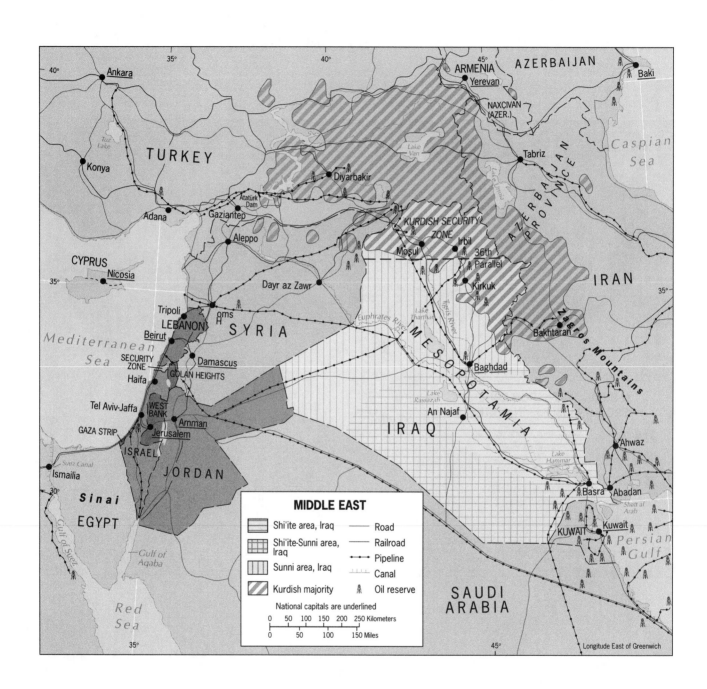

MIDDLE EAST

- Shi'ite area, Iraq
- Shi'ite-Sunni area, Iraq
- Sunni area, Iraq
- Kurdish majority
- Road
- Railroad
- Pipeline
- Canal
- Oil reserve

National capitals are underlined

0 50 100 150 200 250 Kilometers
0 50 100 150 Miles

Longitude East of Greenwich

FIGURE 6-13

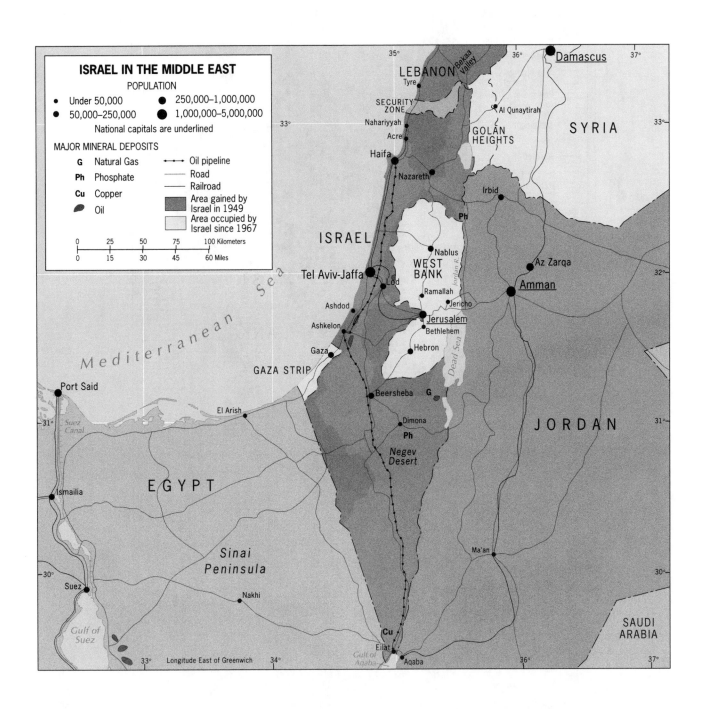

ISRAEL IN THE MIDDLE EAST

POPULATION

- Under 50,000
- 50,000–250,000
- 250,000–1,000,000
- 1,000,000–5,000,000

National capitals are underlined

MAJOR MINERAL DEPOSITS

G Natural Gas
Ph Phosphate
Cu Copper
Oil

Oil pipeline
Road
Railroad

Area gained by Israel in 1949
Area occupied by Israel since 1967

0   25   50   75   100 Kilometers
0   15   30   45   60 Miles

FIGURE 6-14

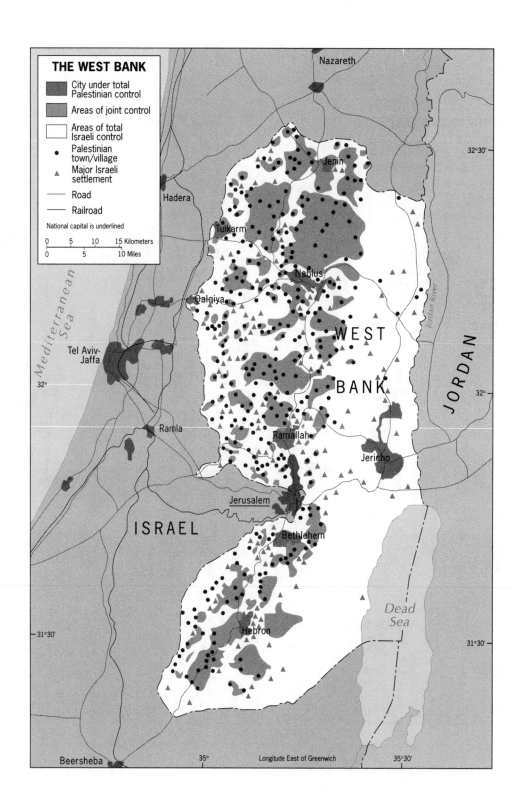

THE WEST BANK

- City under total Palestinian control
- Areas of joint control
- Areas of total Israeli control
- Palestinian town/village
- ▲ Major Israeli settlement
- Road
- Railroad

National capital is underlined

0 5 10 15 Kilometers
0 5 10 Miles

Mediterranean Sea

Nazareth

Hadera

Jenin

Tulkarm

Nablus

Qalqiya

WEST

Tel Aviv-Jaffa

BANK

JORDAN

Ramla

Ramallah

Jericho

Jordan River

Jerusalem

Bethlehem

ISRAEL

Dead Sea

Hebron

Beersheba

35°   Longitude East of Greenwich   35°30'

32°30'

32°

31°30'

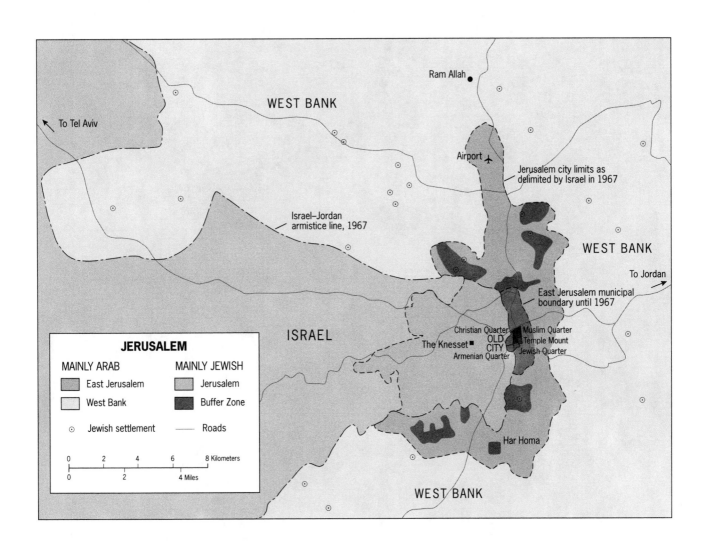

Ram Allah

WEST BANK

To Tel Aviv

Airport

Jerusalem city limits as delimited by Israel in 1967

Israel–Jordan armistice line, 1967

WEST BANK

To Jordan

East Jerusalem municipal boundary until 1967

ISRAEL

Christian Quarter   Muslim Quarter
The Knesset ■   OLD   Temple Mount
CITY   Jewish Quarter
Armenian Quarter

Har Homa

WEST BANK

JERUSALEM

MAINLY ARAB   MAINLY JEWISH

　East Jerusalem   Jerusalem

　West Bank   Buffer Zone

⊙ Jewish settlement   ‥‥‥ Roads

0   2   4   6   8 Kilometers

0   2   4 Miles

FIGURE 6-16

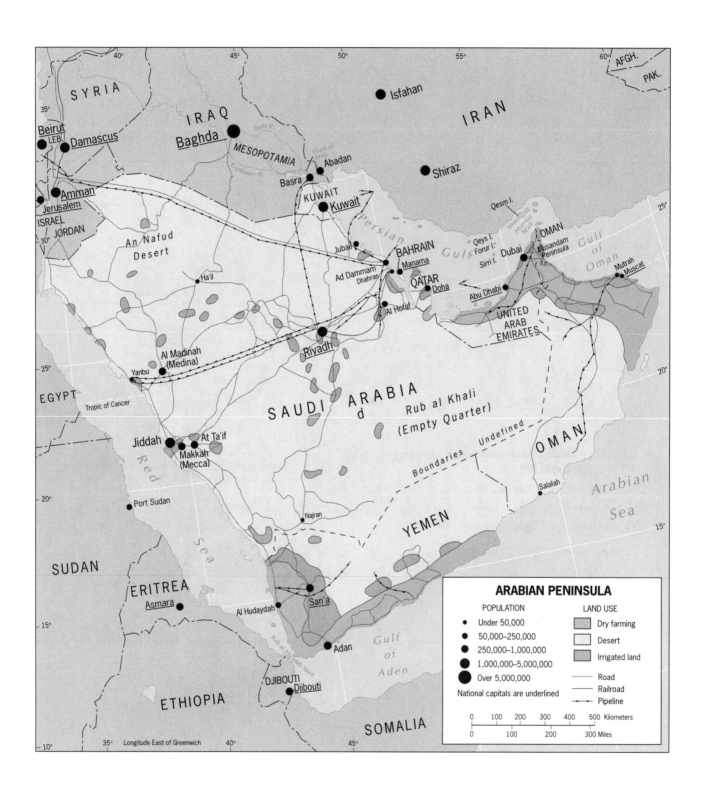

ARABIAN PENINSULA

POPULATION

- Under 50,000
- 50,000–250,000
- 250,000–1,000,000
- 1,000,000–5,000,000
- Over 5,000,000

National capitals are underlined

LAND USE

- Dry farming
- Desert
- Irrigated land

— Road
— Railroad
•–•– Pipeline

| 0 | 100 | 200 | 300 | 400 | 500 | Kilometers |
| 0 | 100 | | 200 | | 300 Miles | |

FIGURE 6-17

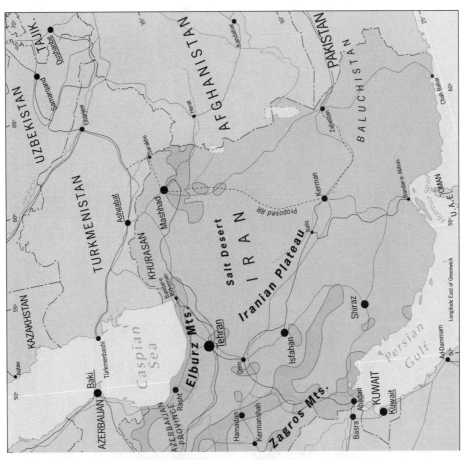

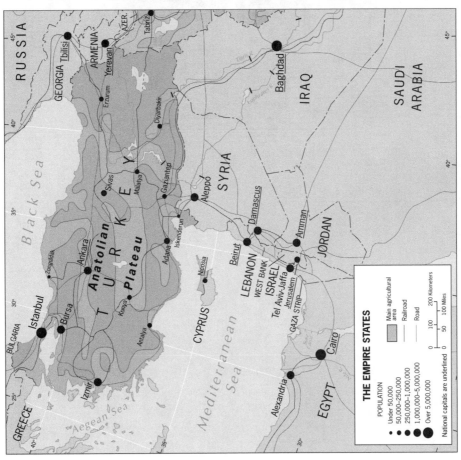

125

FIGURE 6-18

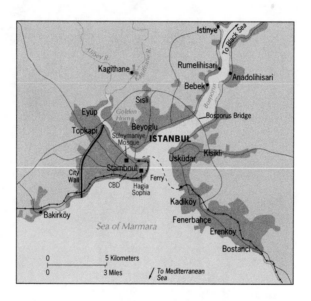

ISTANBUL

FIGURE 6-19

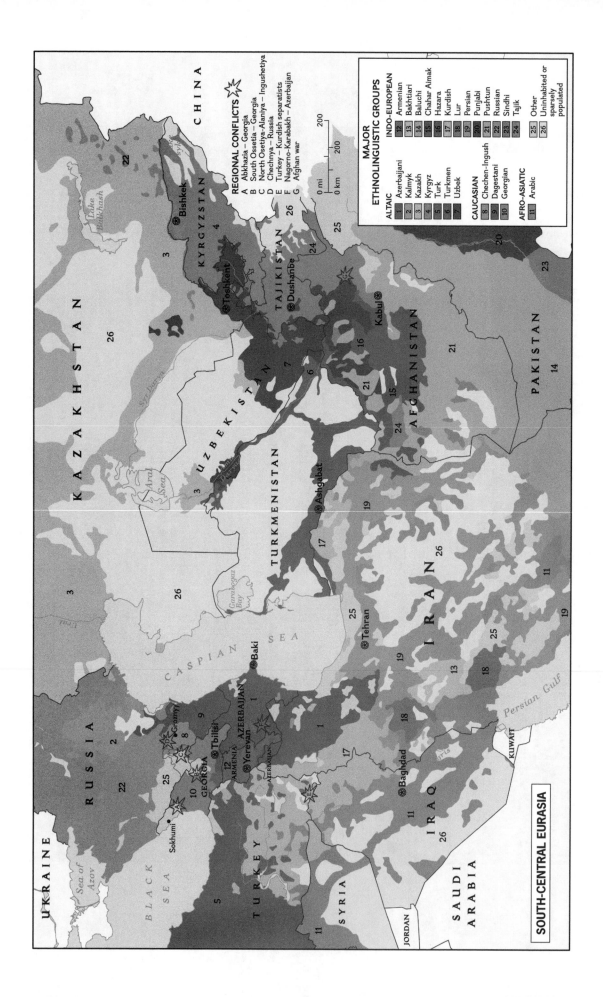

SOUTH-CENTRAL EURASIA

128

FIGURE 6-20

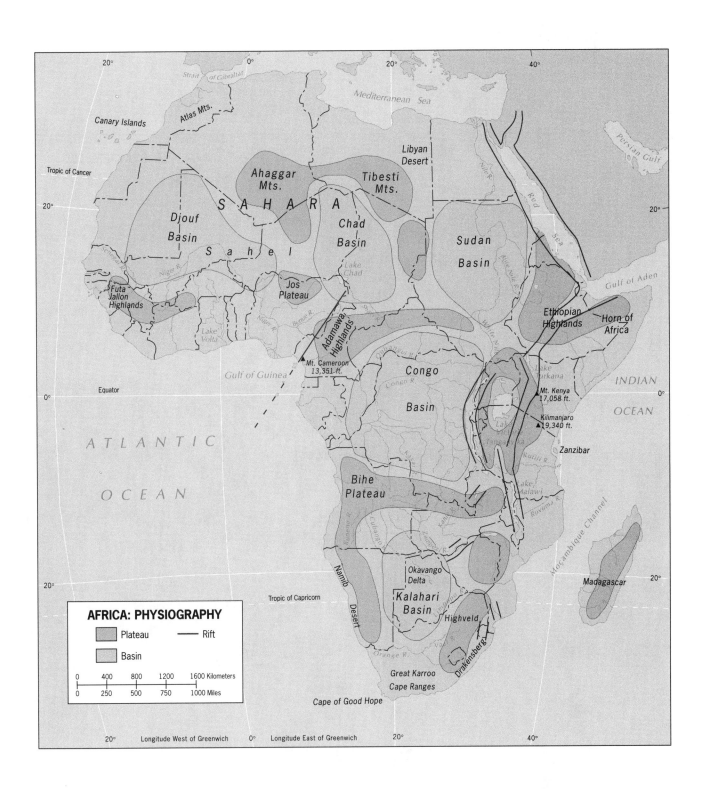

AFRICA: PHYSIOGRAPHY

Plateau   Rift

Basin

| 0 | 400 | 800 | 1200 | 1600 Kilometers |
| 0 | 250 | 500 | 750 | 1000 Miles |

FIGURE 7-2

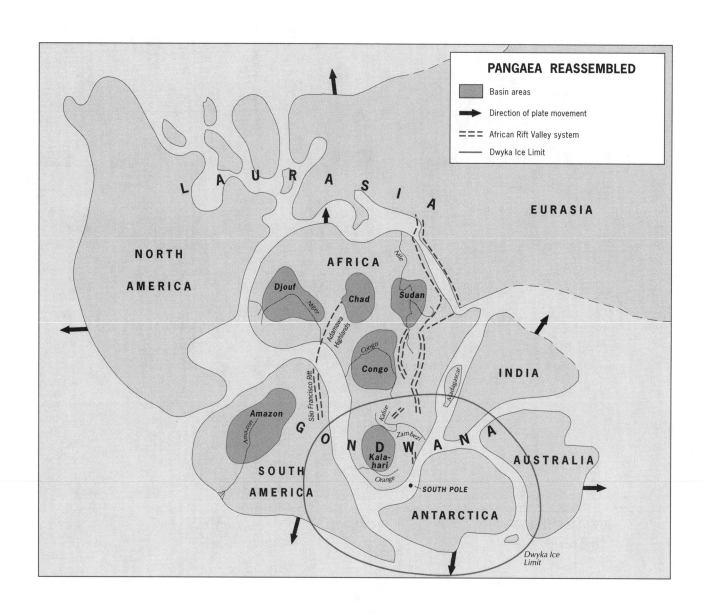

PANGAEA REASSEMBLED

Basin areas

Direction of plate movement

African Rift Valley system

Dwyka Ice Limit

130

FIGURE 7-3

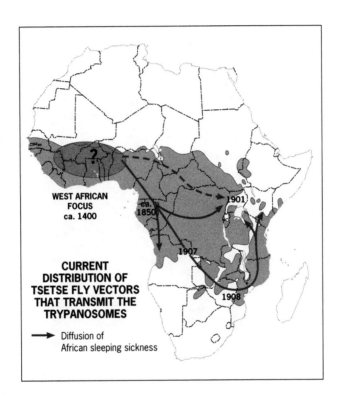

WEST AFRICAN
FOCUS
ca. 1400

ca.
1850

1901

1907

1908

**CURRENT
DISTRIBUTION OF
TSETSE FLY VECTORS
THAT TRANSMIT THE
TRYPANOSOMES**

→ Diffusion of
African sleeping sickness

FIGURE 7-4

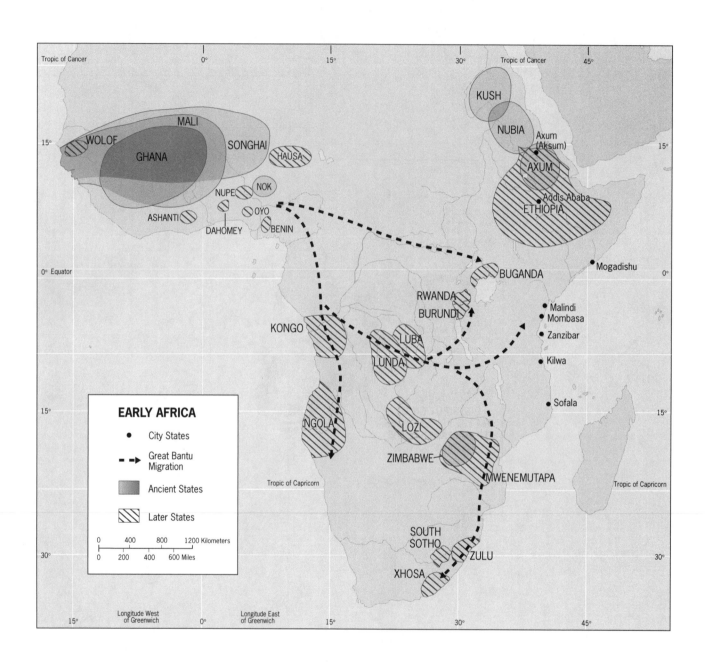

EARLY AFRICA

- **●** City States
- **- - ▶** Great Bantu Migration
- Ancient States
- Later States

| 0 | 400 | 800 | 1200 Kilometers |
| 0 | 200 | 400 | 600 Miles |

Tropic of Cancer

KUSH

NUBIA

Axum (Aksum)

AXUM

Addis Ababa

ETHIOPIA

WOLOF

MALI

GHANA

SONGHAI

HAUSA

NUPE

NOK

ASHANTI

DAHOMEY

OYO

BENIN

KONGO

BUGANDA

RWANDA

BURUNDI

LUBA

LUNDA

Mogadishu

Malindi

Mombasa

Zanzibar

Kilwa

Sofala

NGOLA

LOZI

ZIMBABWE

MWENEMUTAPA

SOUTH SOTHO

XHOSA

ZULU

Tropic of Cancer

Equator

Tropic of Capricorn

Longitude West of Greenwich

Longitude East of Greenwich

FIGURE 7-5

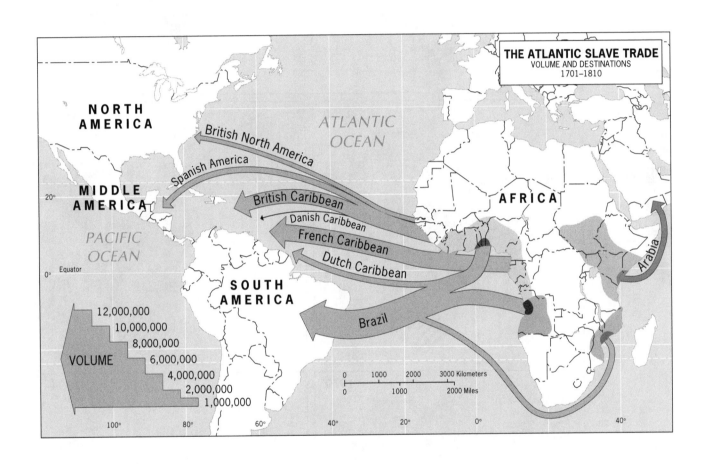

THE ATLANTIC SLAVE TRADE
VOLUME AND DESTINATIONS
1701–1810

NORTH AMERICA

ATLANTIC OCEAN

British North America

Spanish America

MIDDLE AMERICA

British Caribbean

Danish Caribbean

French Caribbean

Dutch Caribbean

PACIFIC OCEAN

Equator

AFRICA

Arabia

SOUTH AMERICA

Brazil

VOLUME

12,000,000
10,000,000
8,000,000
6,000,000
4,000,000
2,000,000
1,000,000

0   1000   2000   3000 Kilometers
0   1000   2000 Miles

100°   80°   60°   40°   20°   0°   40°

FIGURE 7-6

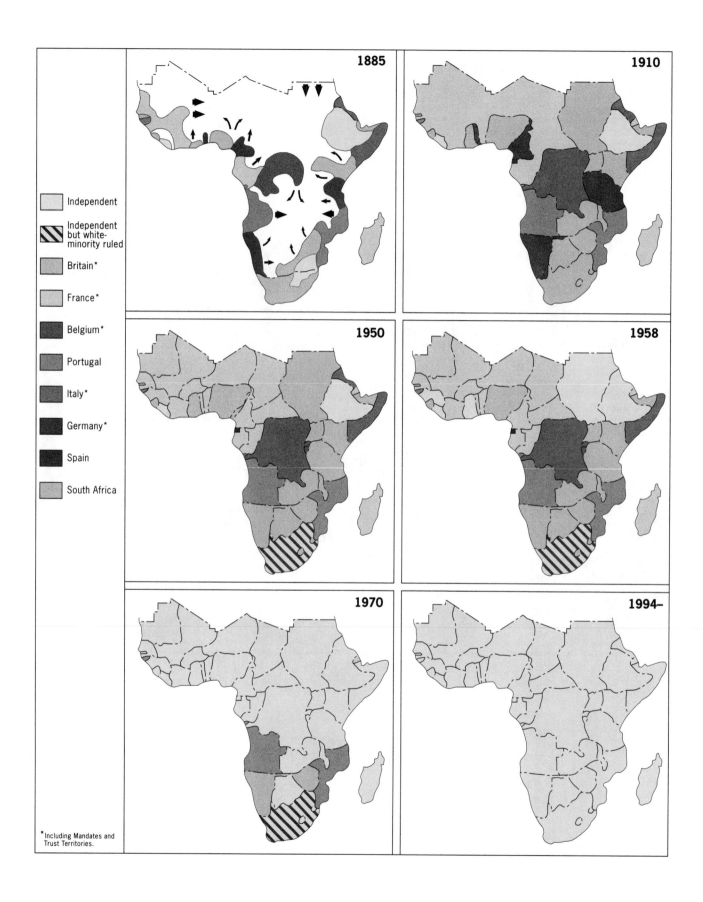

Legend

- Independent
- Independent but white-minority ruled
- Britain*
- France*
- Belgium*
- Portugal
- Italy*
- Germany*
- Spain
- South Africa

*Including Mandates and Trust Territories.

1885

1910

1950

1958

1970

1994–

FIGURE 7-7

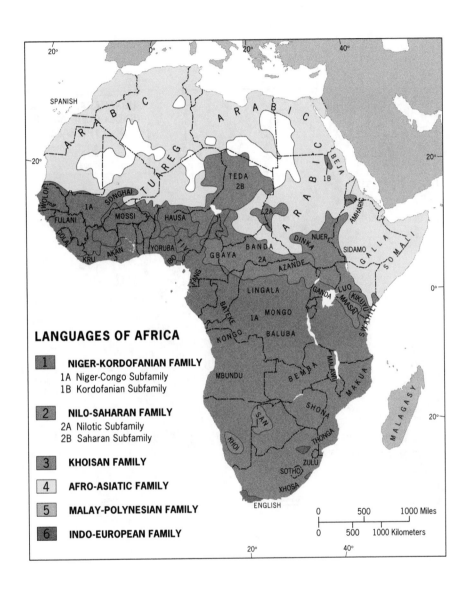

LANGUAGES OF AFRICA

1 **NIGER-KORDOFANIAN FAMILY**
1A Niger-Congo Subfamily
1B Kordofanian Subfamily

2 **NILO-SAHARAN FAMILY**
2A Nilotic Subfamily
2B Saharan Subfamily

3 **KHOISAN FAMILY**

4 **AFRO-ASIATIC FAMILY**

5 **MALAY-POLYNESIAN FAMILY**

6 **INDO-EUROPEAN FAMILY**

FIGURE 7-8

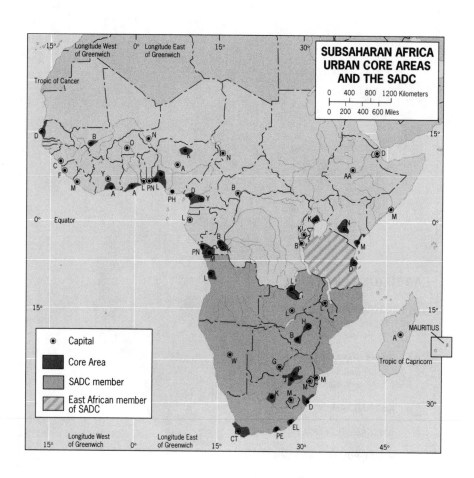

FIGURE 7-9

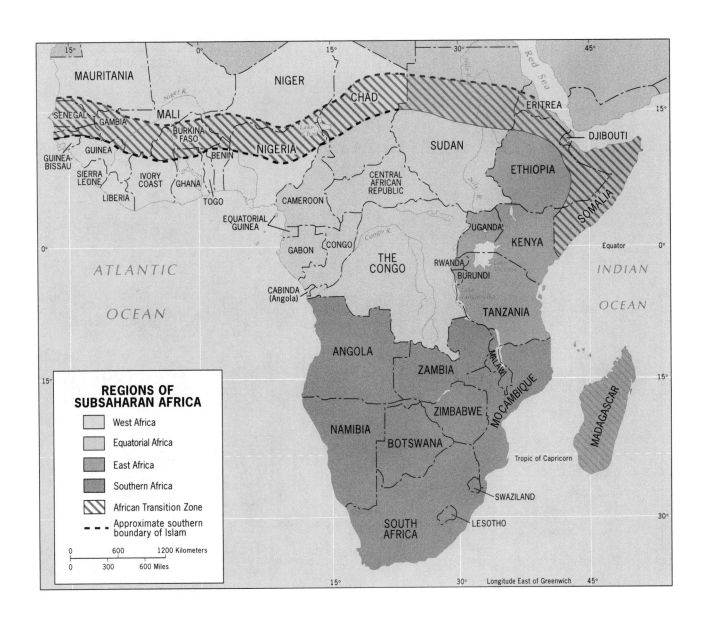

REGIONS OF SUBSAHARAN AFRICA

- West Africa
- Equatorial Africa
- East Africa
- Southern Africa
- African Transition Zone
- Approximate southern boundary of Islam

0   600   1200 Kilometers
0   300   600 Miles

137

FIGURE 7-10

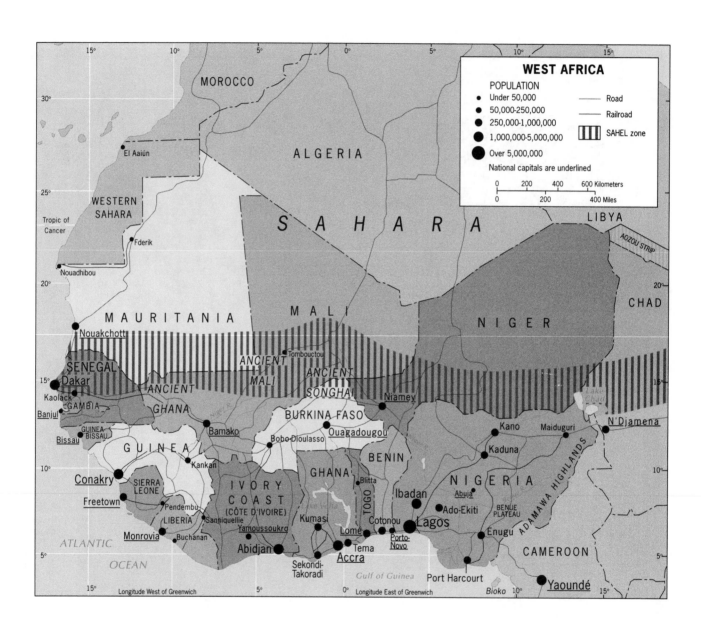

138

FIGURE 7-11

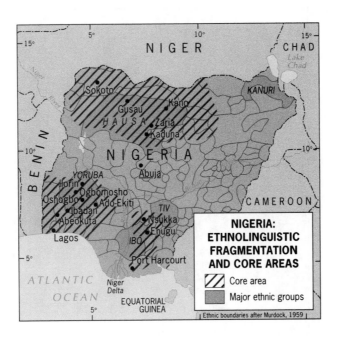

NIGERIA: ETHNOLINGUISTIC FRAGMENTATION AND CORE AREAS

Core area

Major ethnic groups

Ethnic boundaries after Murdock, 1959

FIGURE 7-12

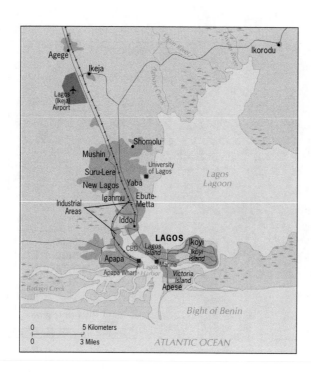

LAGOS

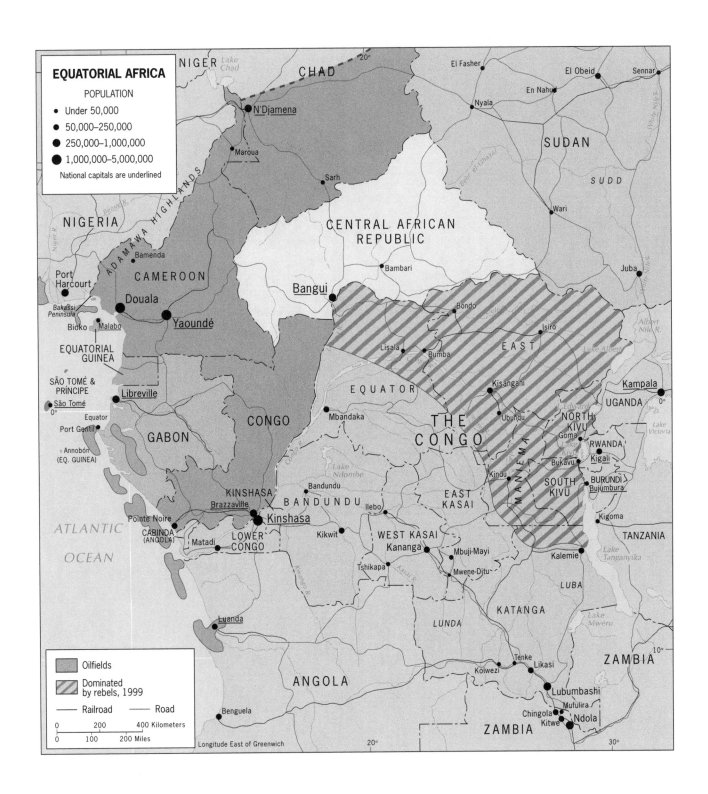

EQUATORIAL AFRICA

POPULATION

- • Under 50,000
- • 50,000–250,000
- • 250,000–1,000,000
- • 1,000,000–5,000,000

National capitals are underlined

Oilfields

Dominated by rebels, 1999

Railroad   Road

0   200   400 Kilometers

0   100   200 Miles

NIGER

Lake Chad

CHAD

20°

El Fasher

El Obeid

Sennar

N'Djamena

Nyala

En Nahud

SUDAN

SUDD

Maroua

Sarh

Wari

CENTRAL AFRICAN REPUBLIC

Bambari

Bahr el-Ghazal

White Nile R.

NIGERIA

Bamenda

Beneue R.

ADAMAWA HIGHLANDS

CAMEROON

Juba

Bangui

Bondo

Isiro

Albert Nile R.

Port Harcourt

Niger R.

Douala

Lisala

EAST

Bumba

Lake Albert

Bakassi Peninsula

Yaoundé

Kampala

Bioko   Malabo

EQUATOR

Kisangani

UGANDA

0°

EQUATORIAL GUINEA

Mbandaka

Ubundu

NORTH KIVU

Lake Victoria

SÃO TOMÉ & PRÍNCIPE

THE CONGO

Goma

Lake Edward

São Tomé

Libreville

Congo R.

RWANDA

0°

Equator

Bukavu

Kigali

Port Gentil

GABON

CONGO

Kindu

MANIEMA

SOUTH KIVU

BURUNDI

Bujumbura

Annobón (EQ. GUINEA)

Lake Ndombe

Kigoma

KINSHASA

Bandundu

EAST KASAI

TANZANIA

Brazzaville

BANDUNDU

Ilebo

Pointe Noire

Kinshasa

Kikwit

Lake Tanganyika

ATLANTIC OCEAN

CABINDA (ANGOLA)

LOWER CONGO

WEST KASAI

Kalemie

Matadi

Kananga

Mbuji-Mayi

Tshikapa

Kasai R.

Mwene-Ditu

LUBA

Kwango R.

KATANGA

LUNDA

Lake Mweru

Luanda

ANGOLA

Tenke

Likasi

ZAMBIA

10°

Kolwezi

Benguela

Lubumbashi

Mufulira

Chingola

Ndola

ZAMBIA

Kitwe

Longitude East of Greenwich   20°   30°

FIGURE 7-13

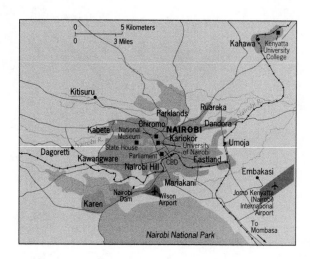

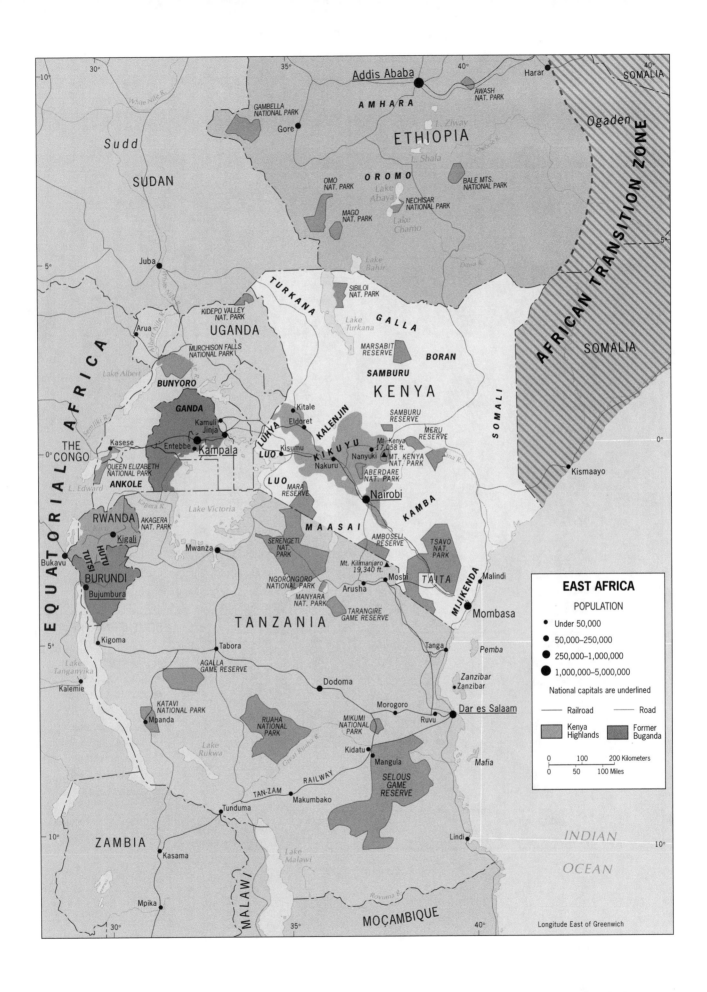

FIGURE 7-14

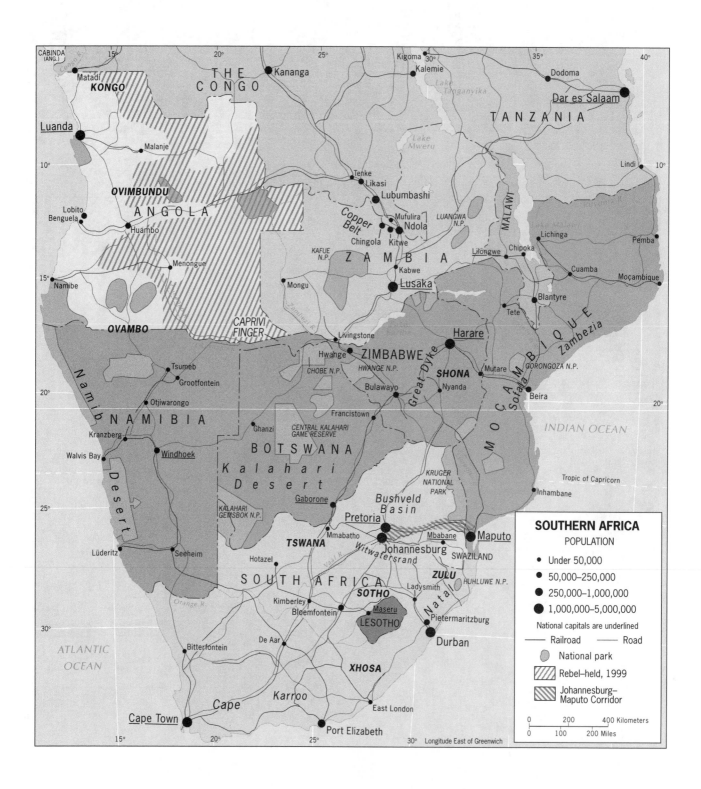

SOUTHERN AFRICA

POPULATION

- Under 50,000
- 50,000–250,000
- 250,000–1,000,000
- 1,000,000–5,000,000

National capitals are underlined

—— Railroad   —— Road

National park

Rebel-held, 1999

Johannesburg–
Maputo Corridor

| 0 | 200 | 400 Kilometers |
| 0 | 100 | 200 Miles |

FIGURE 7-15

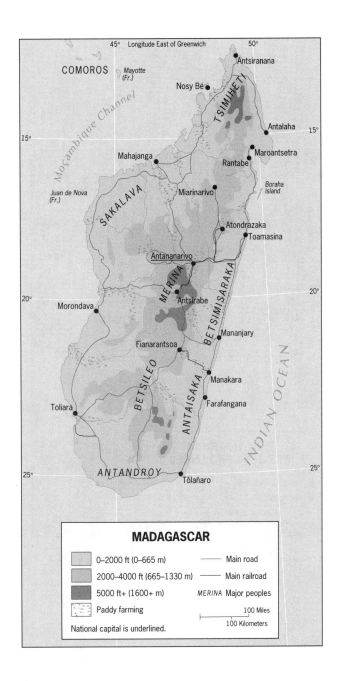

MADAGASCAR

0–2000 ft (0–665 m)	Main road
2000–4000 ft (665–1330 m)	Main railroad
5000 ft+ (1600+ m)	*MERINA* Major peoples
Paddy farming	

National capital is underlined.

100 Miles

100 Kilometers

145

FIGURE 7-16

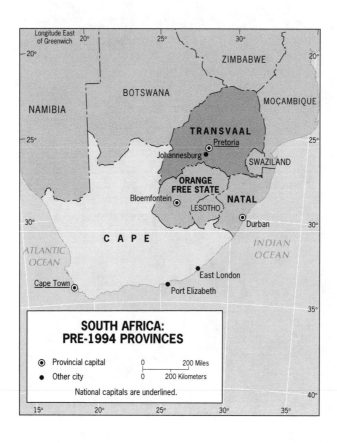

**SOUTH AFRICA:
PRE-1994 PROVINCES**

◉ Provincial capital

● Other city

National capitals are underlined.

0 — 200 Miles
0 — 200 Kilometers

FIGURE 7-17

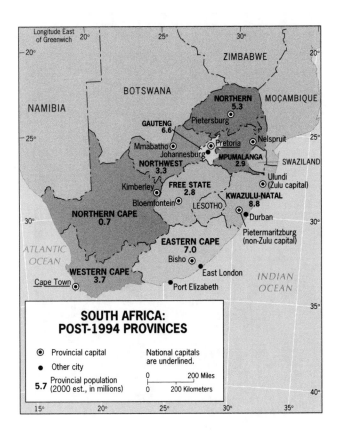

SOUTH AFRICA:
POST-1994 PROVINCES

⊙ Provincial capital

● Other city

5.7 Provincial population
(2000 est., in millions)

National capitals
are underlined.

0   200 Miles

0   200 Kilometers

FIGURE 7-18

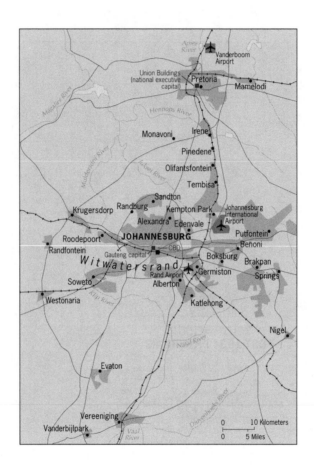

JOHANNESBURG

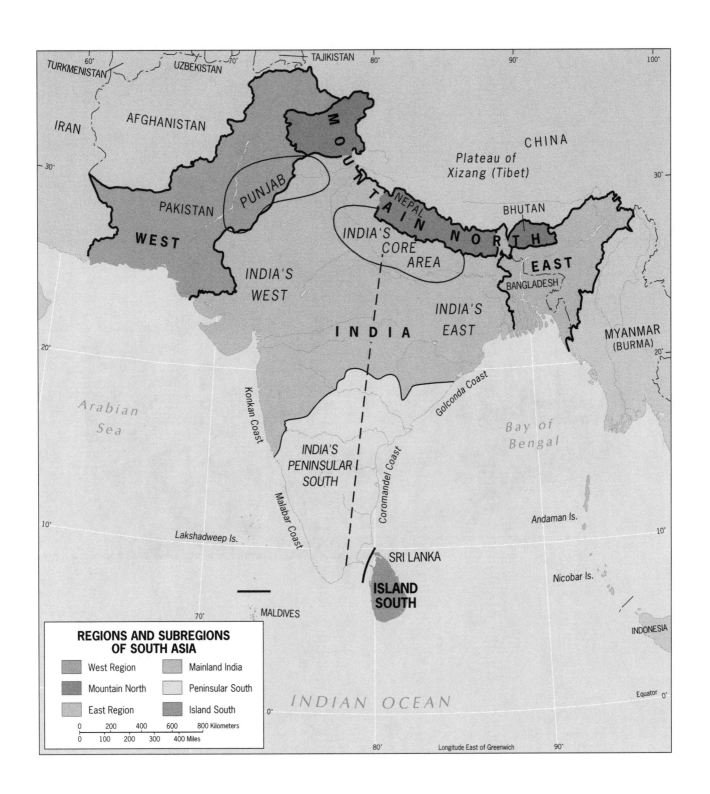

FIGURE 8-2

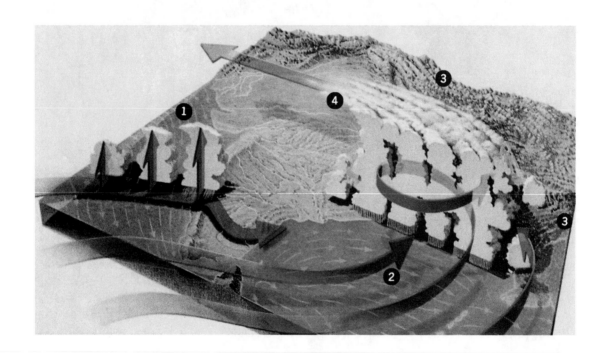

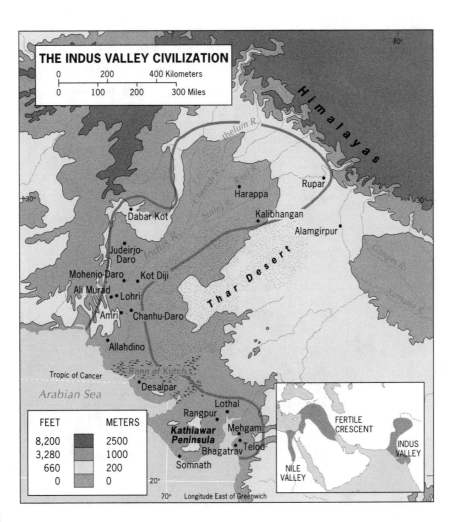

THE INDUS VALLEY CIVILIZATION

0   200   400 Kilometers
0 100   200   300 Miles

Himalayas

thelum R.

Chenab R.

Ravi R.

Sutlej R.

Indus R.

Rupar
Harappa
Kalibhangan
Alamgirpur
Dabar Kot
Judeirjo-Daro
Mohenjo-Daro   Kot Diji
Ali Murad Lohri
Amri   Chanhu-Daro

Thar Desert

Ganges R.
Yamuna R.

Allahdino

Tropic of Cancer
Rann of Kutch
Arabian Sea
Desalpar
Lothal
Rangpur
Kathiawar Peninsula   Mehgam
Bhagatrav Telod
Somnath

FEET | METERS
8,200 | 2500
3,280 | 1000
660 | 200
0 | 0

80°
30°
30°
20°
70°   Longitude East of Greenwich

FERTILE CRESCENT
INDUS VALLEY
NILE VALLEY

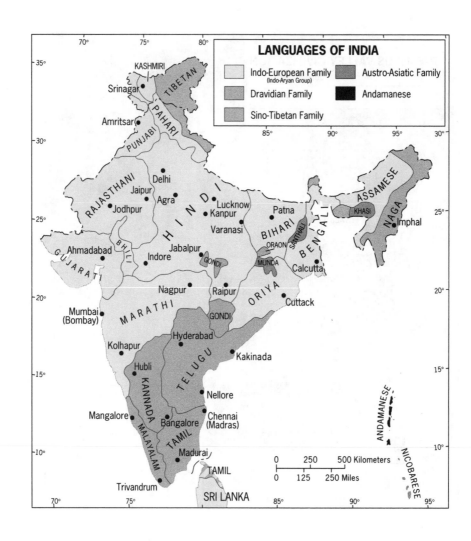

LANGUAGES OF INDIA

Indo-European Family (Indo-Aryan Group)		Austro-Asiatic Family
Dravidian Family		Andamanese
Sino-Tibetan Family		

FIGURE 8-5

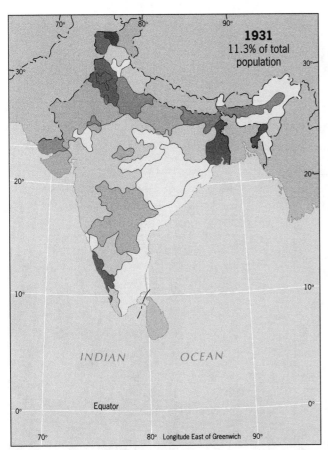

1931
11.3% of total population

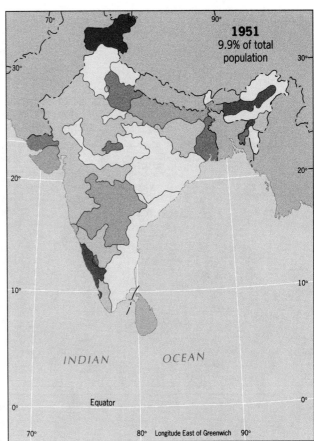

1951
9.9% of total population

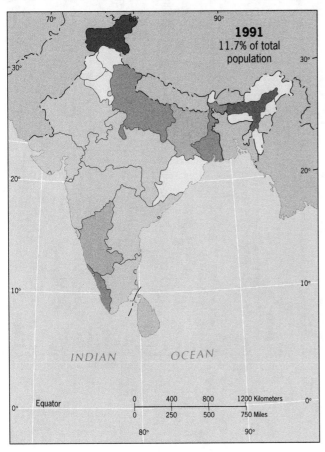

1991
11.7% of total population

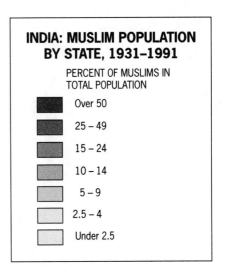

INDIA: MUSLIM POPULATION BY STATE, 1931–1991

PERCENT OF MUSLIMS IN TOTAL POPULATION

Over 50

25 – 49

15 – 24

10 – 14

5 – 9

2.5 – 4

Under 2.5

FIGURE 8-6

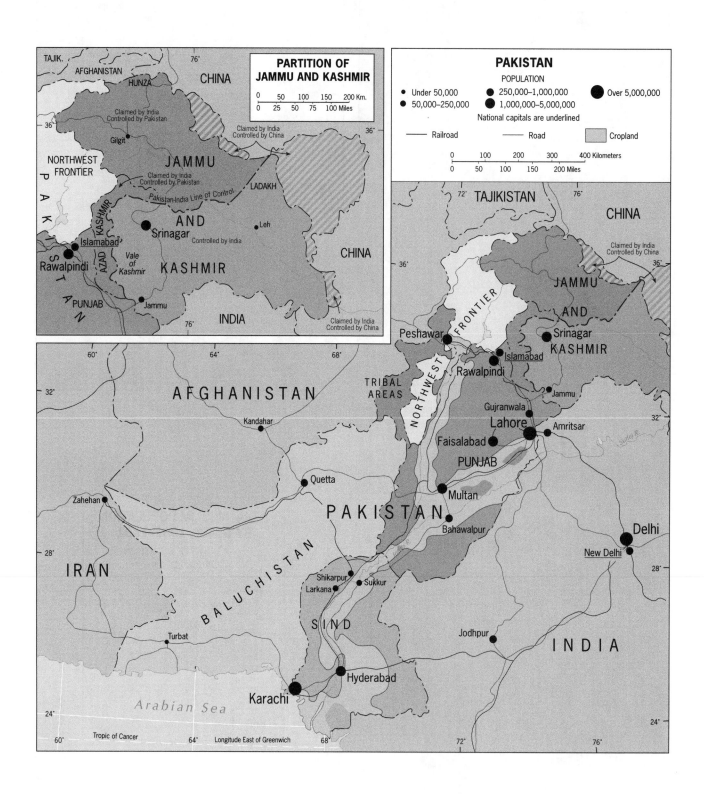

PARTITION OF JAMMU AND KASHMIR

TAJIK.
AFGHANISTAN
CHINA
HUNZA
Claimed by India
Controlled by Pakistan
Gilgit
NORTHWEST FRONTIER
JAMMU
Claimed by India
Controlled by China
LADAKH
Claimed by India
Controlled by Pakistan
Pakistan-India Line of Control
CHINA
Srinagar
Leh
AND
Controlled by India
Islamabad
CHINA
Rawalpindi
Vale of Kashmir
KASHMIR
PUNJAB
Jammu
INDIA
Claimed by India
Controlled by China

0 50 100 150 200 Km.
0 25 50 75 100 Miles

PAKISTAN
POPULATION
● Under 50,000   ● 250,000–1,000,000   ● Over 5,000,000
● 50,000–250,000   ● 1,000,000–5,000,000
National capitals are underlined
—— Railroad   —— Road   Cropland

0 100 200 300 400 Kilometers
0 50 100 150 200 Miles

TAJIKISTAN
CHINA
Claimed by India
Controlled by China
NORTHWEST FRONTIER
JAMMU
Peshawar
AND
Srinagar
Islamabad
KASHMIR
Rawalpindi
TRIBAL AREAS
Jammu
Gujranwala
Lahore
Amritsar
Faisalabad
PUNJAB
AFGHANISTAN
Kandahar
Multan
Delhi
PAKISTAN
Bahawalpur
New Delhi
Quetta
Zahehan
IRAN
BALUCHISTAN
Shikarpur
Sukkur
Larkana
SIND
Jodhpur
Turbat
INDIA
Hyderabad
Karachi
Arabian Sea
Tropic of Cancer
Longitude East of Greenwich

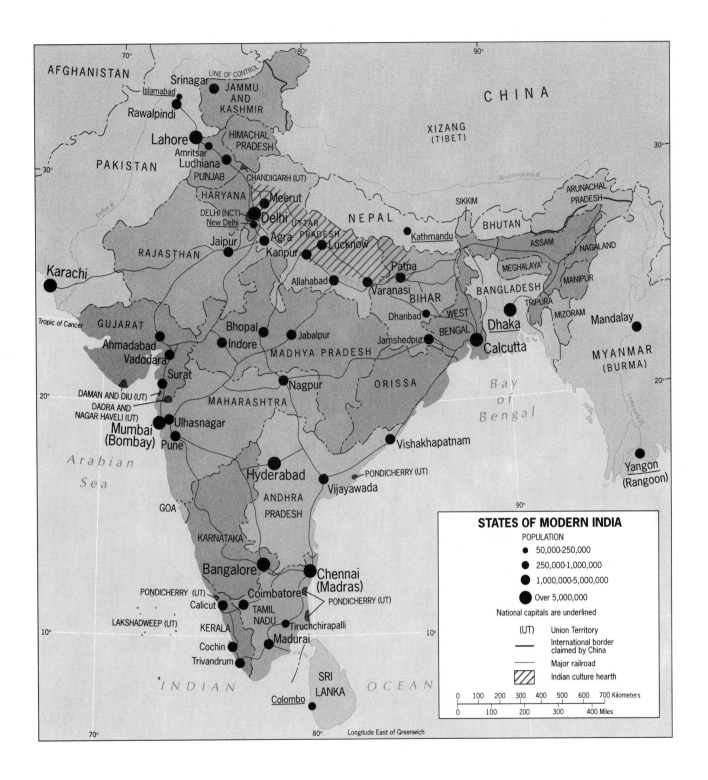

STATES OF MODERN INDIA

POPULATION

- ● 50,000-250,000
- ● 250,000-1,000,000
- ● 1,000,000-5,000,000
- ● Over 5,000,000

National capitals are underlined

(UT) Union Territory

—— International border claimed by China

— Major railroad

▨ Indian culture hearth

0   100 200 300 400 500 600 700 Kilometers

0   100   200   300   400 Miles

FIGURE 8-8

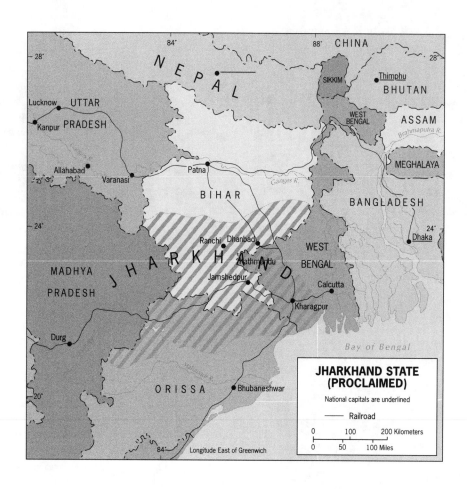

JHARKHAND STATE (PROCLAIMED)

National capitals are underlined

— Railroad

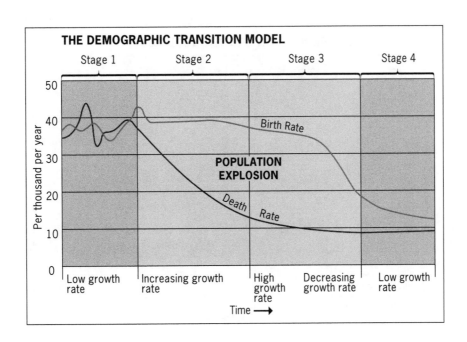

FIGURE 8-10

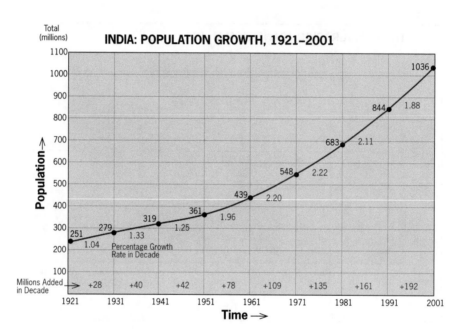

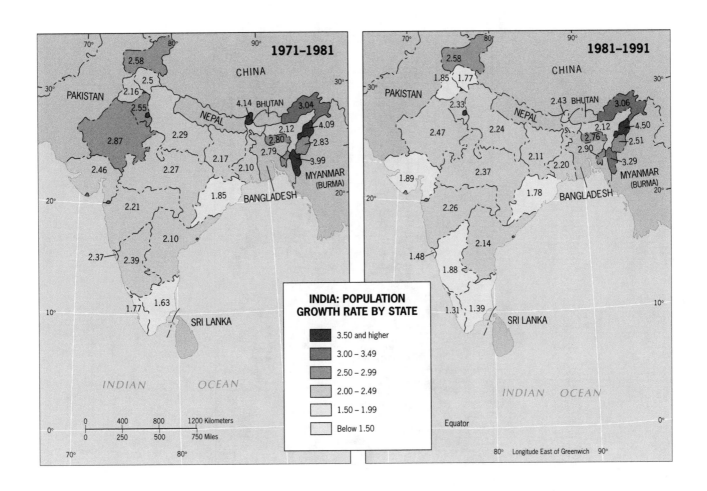

INDIA: POPULATION GROWTH RATE BY STATE

3.50 and higher
3.00 – 3.49
2.50 – 2.99
2.00 – 2.49
1.50 – 1.99
Below 1.50

159

FIGURE 8-12

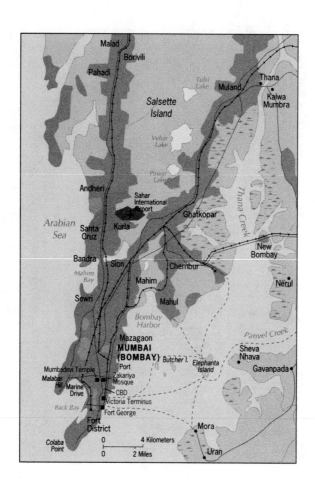

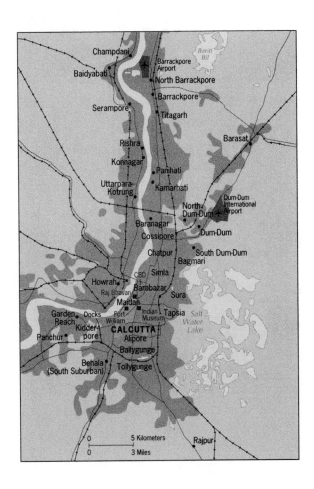

CALCUTTA

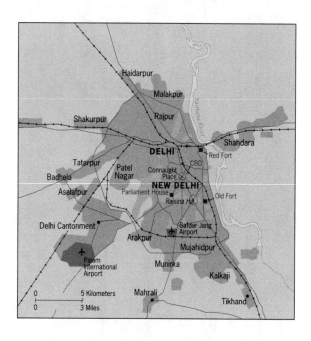

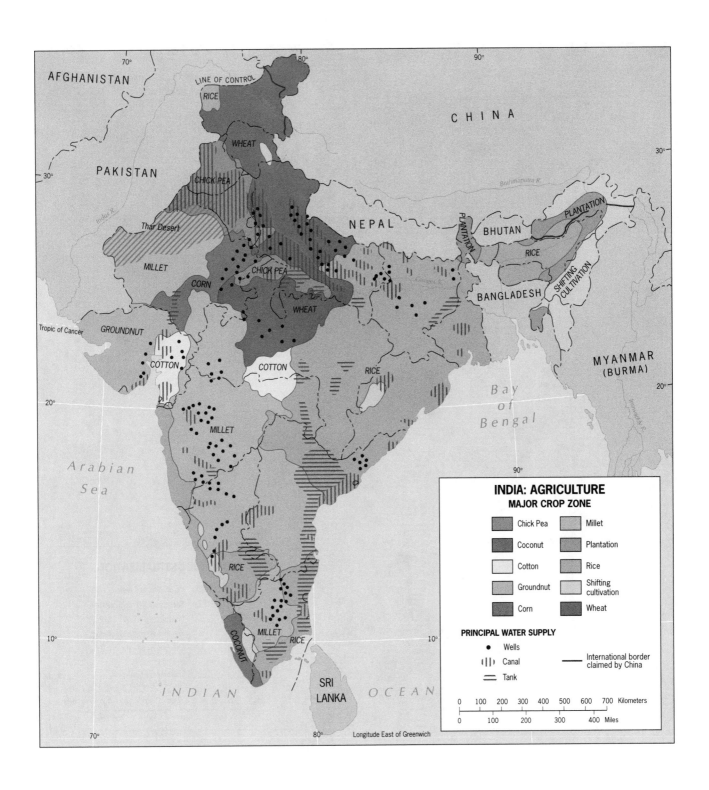

INDIA: AGRICULTURE
MAJOR CROP ZONE

Chick Pea		Millet	
Coconut		Plantation	
Cotton		Rice	
Groundnut		Shifting cultivation	
Corn		Wheat	

PRINCIPAL WATER SUPPLY

- Wells
- Canal
- Tank
- International border claimed by China

0 100 200 300 400 500 600 700 Kilometers

0 100 200 300 400 Miles

FIGURE 8-13

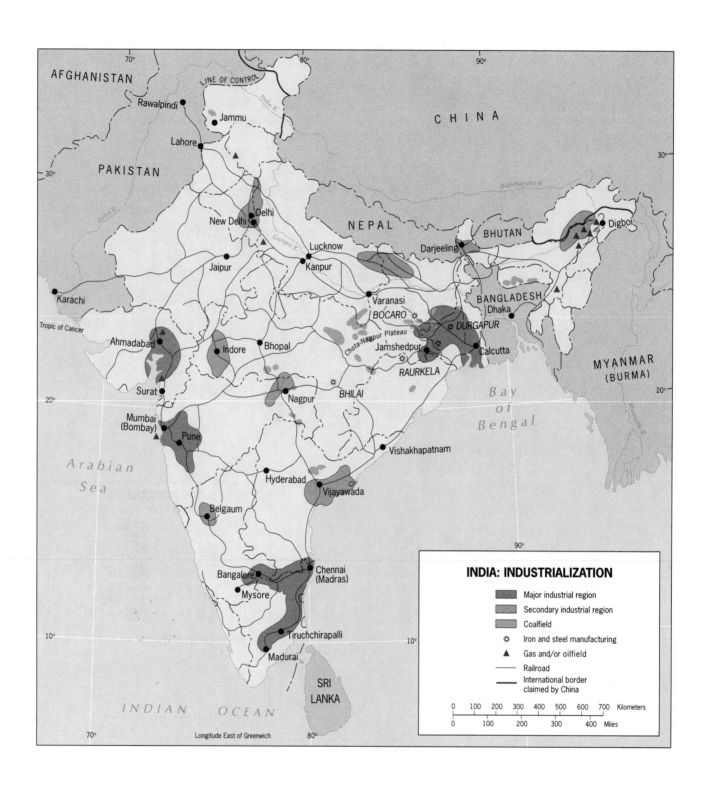

INDIA: INDUSTRIALIZATION

- Major industrial region
- Secondary industrial region
- Coalfield
- ☼ Iron and steel manufacturing
- ▲ Gas and/or oilfield
- Railroad
- International border claimed by China

| 0 | 100 | 200 | 300 | 400 | 500 | 600 | 700 | Kilometers |

| 0 | 100 | 200 | 300 | 400 | Miles |

FIGURE 8-14

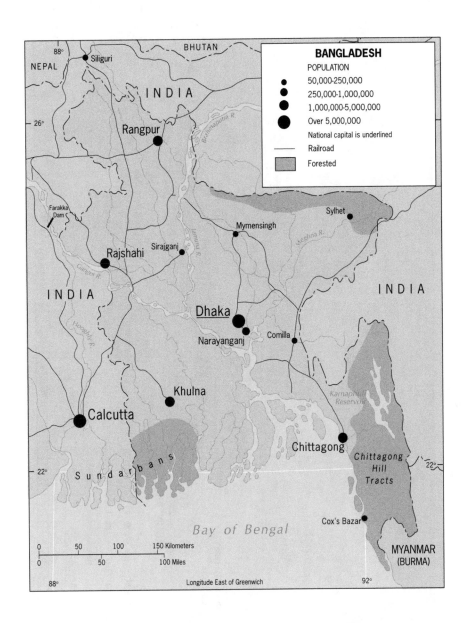

FIGURE 8-15

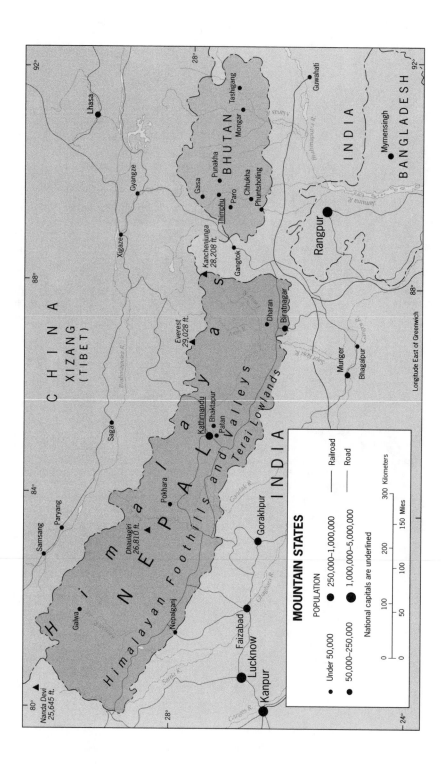

166

FIGURE 8-16

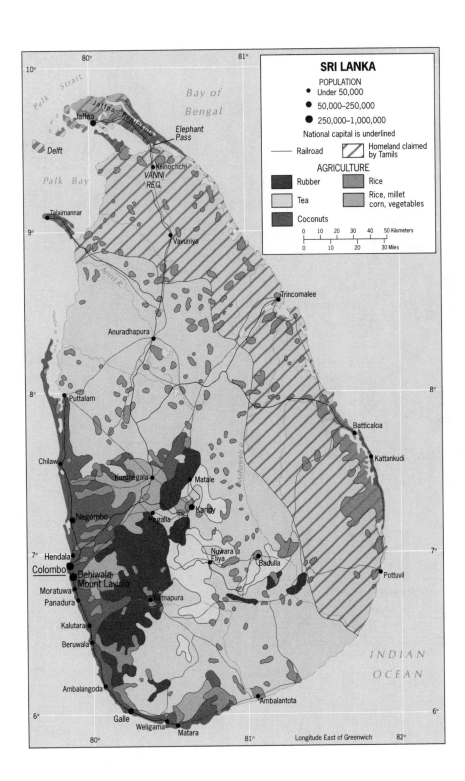

SRI LANKA

POPULATION
- • Under 50,000
- • 50,000–250,000
- • 250,000–1,000,000

National capital is underlined

Railroad   Homeland claimed by Tamils

AGRICULTURE

Rubber   Rice

Tea   Rice, millet corn, vegetables

Coconuts

0 10 20 30 40 50 Kilometers

0 10 20 30 Miles

FIGURE 8-17

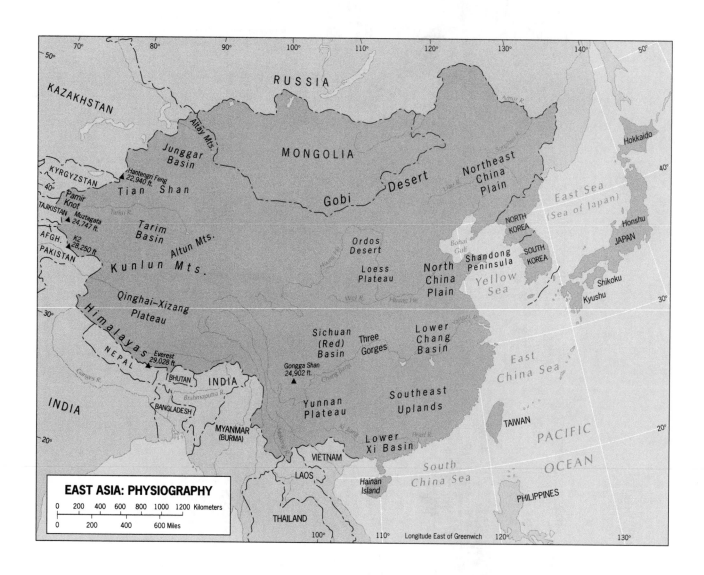

EAST ASIA: PHYSIOGRAPHY

0 200 400 600 800 1000 1200 Kilometers

0 200 400 600 Miles

FIGURE 9-2

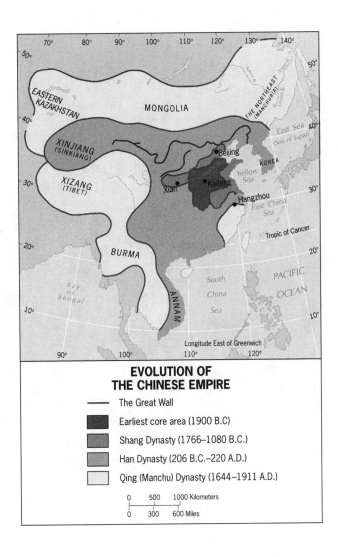

**EVOLUTION OF
THE CHINESE EMPIRE**

—— The Great Wall

Earliest core area (1900 B.C)

Shang Dynasty (1766–1080 B.C.)

Han Dynasty (206 B.C.–220 A.D.)

Qing (Manchu) Dynasty (1644–1911 A.D.)

0   500   1000 Kilometers

0   300   600 Miles

FIGURE 9-3

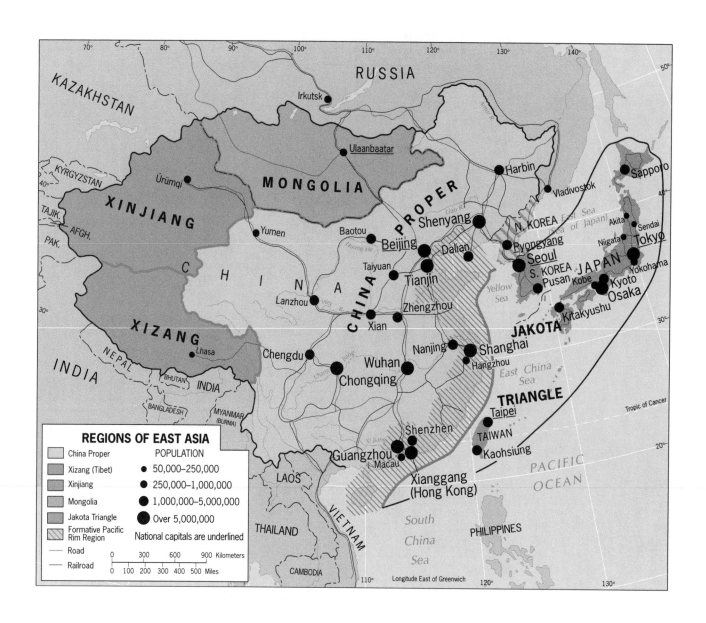

REGIONS OF EAST ASIA

China Proper

Xizang (Tibet)

Xinjiang

Mongolia

Jakota Triangle

Formative Pacific
Rim Region

Road

Railroad

POPULATION

- 50,000–250,000
- 250,000–1,000,000
- 1,000,000–5,000,000
- Over 5,000,000

National capitals are underlined

0   300   600   900 Kilometers

0 100 200 300 400 500 Miles

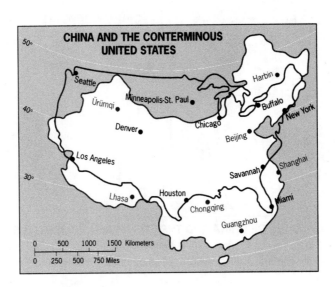

CHINA AND THE CONTERMINOUS UNITED STATES

FIGURE 9-5

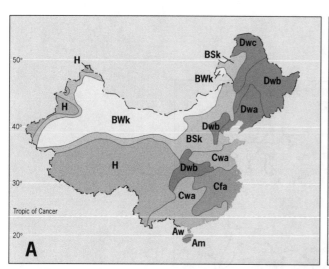

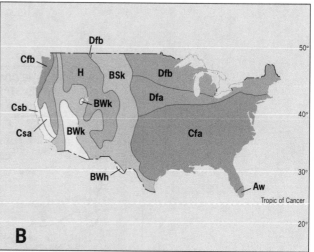

CLIMATES OF CHINA AND THE CONTERMINOUS UNITED STATES
After Köppen-Geiger

A HUMID EQUATORIAL CLIMATE

| Am | Short dry season |
| Aw | Dry winter |

B DRY CLIMATE

| B | Semiarid |
| B | Arid |

h=hot
k=cold

C HUMID TEMPERATE CLIMATE

Cf	No dry season
Cw	Dry winter
Cs	Dry summer

a=hot summer **b**=cool summer **c**=short, cool summer

D HUMID COLD CLIMATE

| Df | No dry season |
| Dw | Dry winter |

H HIGHLAND CLIMATE

| H | Unclassified highlands |

FIGURE 9-6

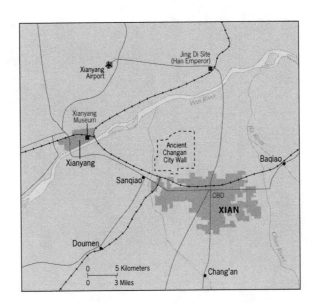

XIAN

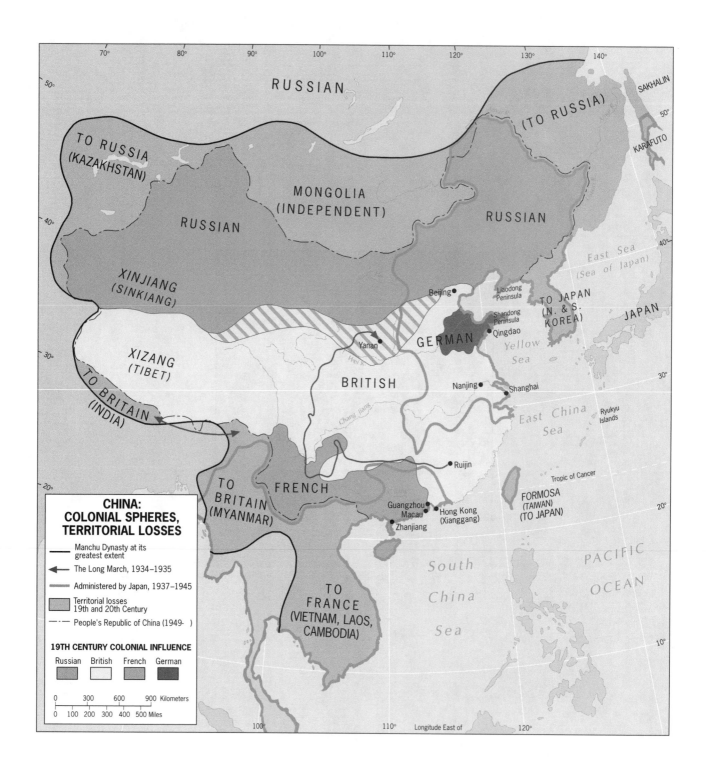

CHINA: COLONIAL SPHERES, TERRITORIAL LOSSES

— Manchu Dynasty at its greatest extent

← The Long March, 1934–1935

▨ Administered by Japan, 1937–1945

■ Territorial losses 19th and 20th Century

–·– People's Republic of China (1949–)

19TH CENTURY COLONIAL INFLUENCE

Russian British French German

0   300   600   900 Kilometers
0 100 200 300 400 500 Miles

TO RUSSIA (KAZAKHSTAN)

RUSSIAN

(TO RUSSIA)

SAKHALIN

KARAFUTO

MONGOLIA (INDEPENDENT)

RUSSIAN

XINJIANG (SINKIANG)

East Sea (Sea of Japan)

Beijing

Liaodong Peninsula

Shandong Peninsula

TO JAPAN (N. & S. KOREA)

JAPAN

XIZANG (TIBET)

TO BRITAIN (INDIA)

Yanan

GERMAN

Qingdao

Yellow Sea

BRITISH

Nanjing

Shanghai

East China Sea

Ryukyu Islands

Chang Jiang

Wei R.

Ruijin

Tropic of Cancer

PACIFIC OCEAN

TO BRITAIN (MYANMAR)

FRENCH

Guangzhou
Macau
Zhanjiang

Hong Kong (Xianggang)

FORMOSA (TAIWAN) (TO JAPAN)

TO FRANCE (VIETNAM, LAOS, CAMBODIA)

South China Sea

100°   110°   Longitude East of   120°

FIGURE 9-7

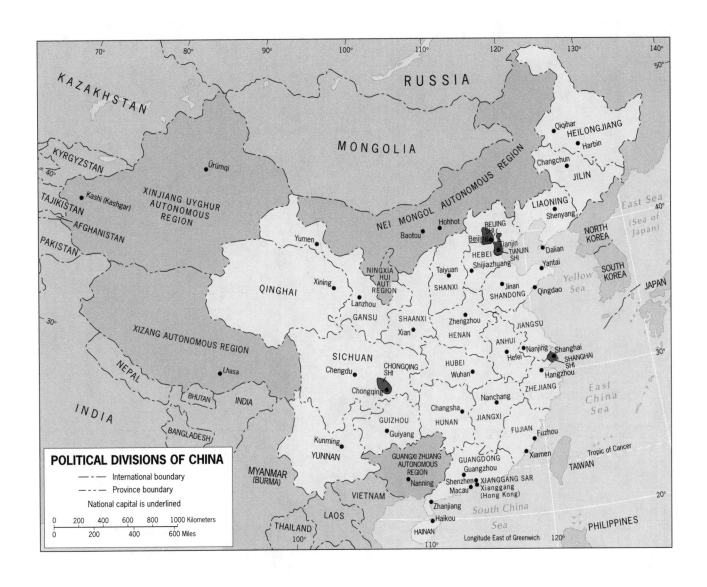

POLITICAL DIVISIONS OF CHINA

— · — · — International boundary
— — — — — Province boundary
National capital is underlined

| 0 | 200 | 400 | 600 | 800 | 1000 Kilometers |
| 0 | 200 | 400 | | 600 Miles |

FIGURE 9-8

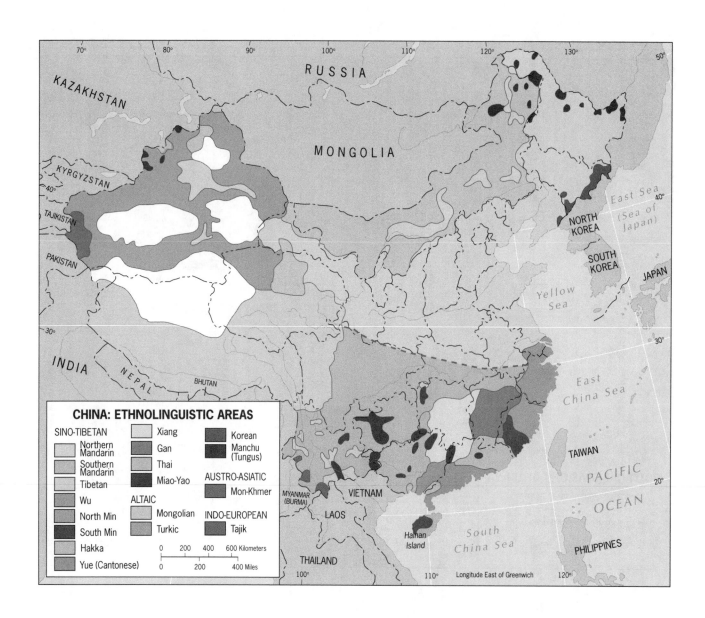

CHINA: ETHNOLINGUISTIC AREAS

SINO-TIBETAN
- Northern Mandarin
- Southern Mandarin
- Tibetan
- Wu
- North Min
- South Min
- Hakka
- Yue (Cantonese)
- Xiang
- Gan
- Thai
- Miao-Yao

ALTAIC
- Mongolian
- Turkic

Korean

Manchu (Tungus)

AUSTRO-ASIATIC
- Mon-Khmer

INDO-EUROPEAN
- Tajik

0   200   400   600 Kilometers

0   200   400 Miles

176

FIGURE 9-9

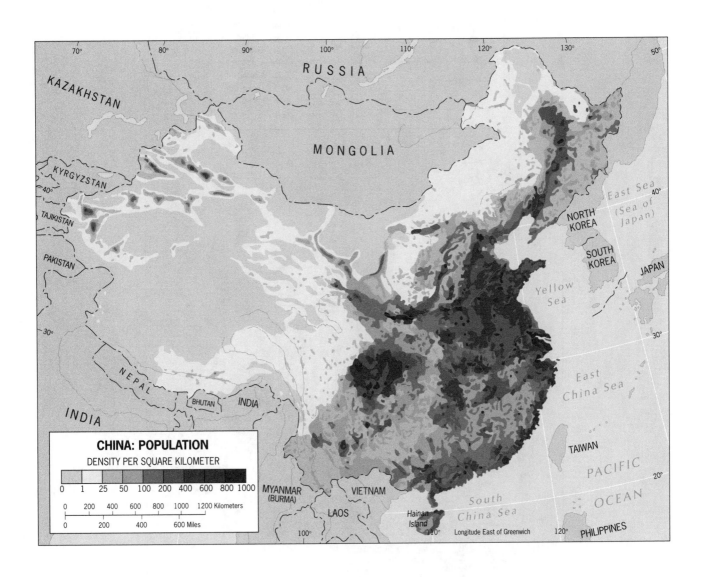

CHINA: POPULATION

DENSITY PER SQUARE KILOMETER

0   1   25   50   100   200   400   600   800   1000

0   200   400   600   800   1000   1200 Kilometers

0   200   400   600 Miles

FIGURE 9-10

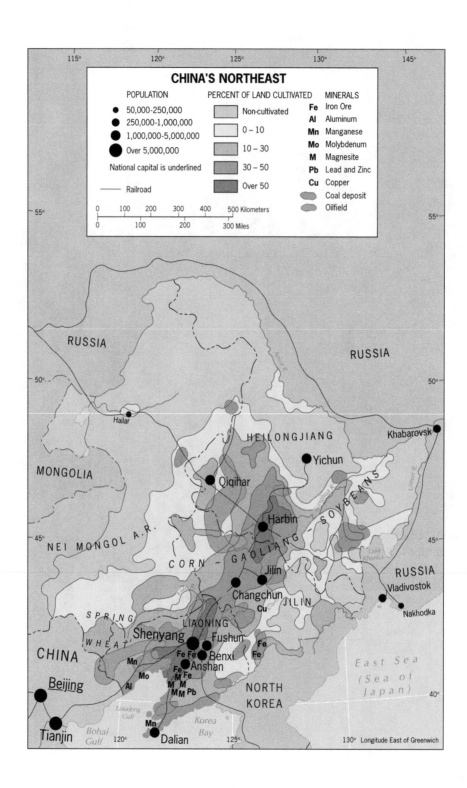

CHINA'S NORTHEAST

FIGURE 9-11

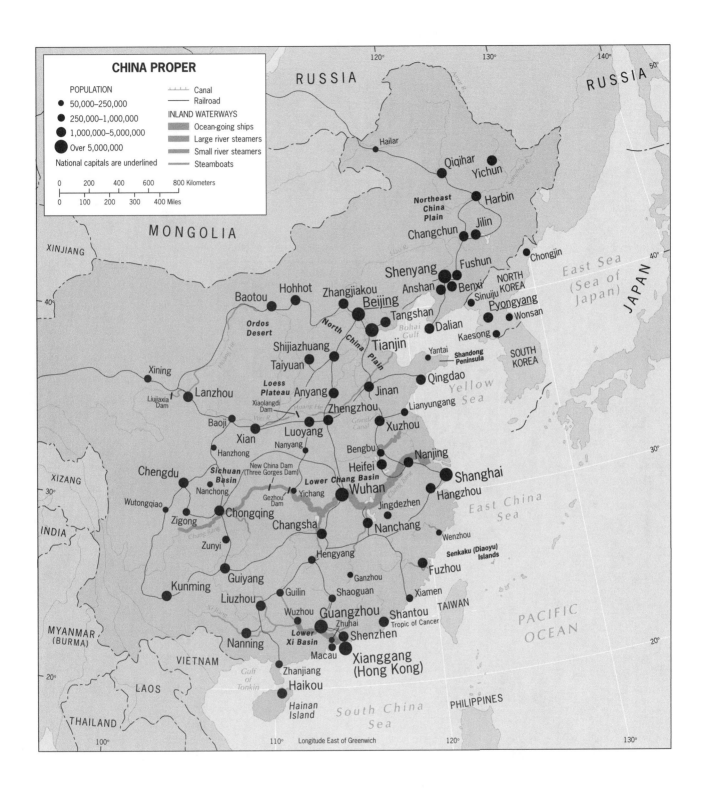

China Proper

CHINA PROPER

POPULATION
- 50,000–250,000
- 250,000–1,000,000
- 1,000,000–5,000,000
- Over 5,000,000

National capitals are underlined

Canal
Railroad

INLAND WATERWAYS
- Ocean-going ships
- Large river steamers
- Small river steamers
- Steamboats

0   200   400   600   800 Kilometers
0   100   200   300   400 Miles

FIGURE 9-12

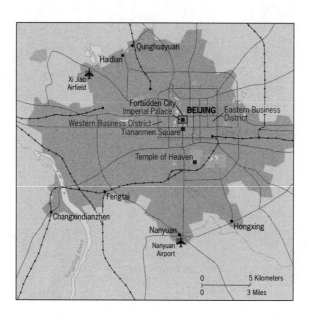

180

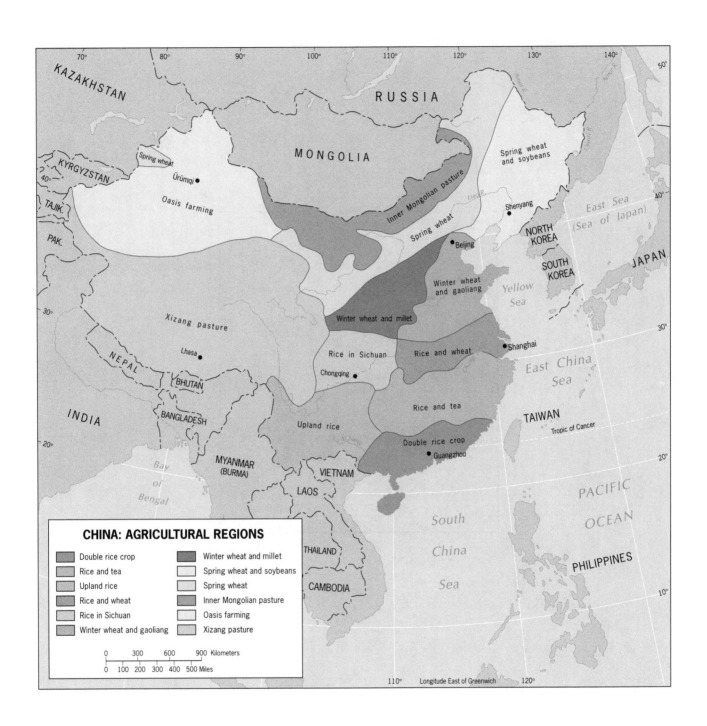

CHINA: AGRICULTURAL REGIONS

- Double rice crop
- Rice and tea
- Upland rice
- Rice and wheat
- Rice in Sichuan
- Winter wheat and gaoliang
- Winter wheat and millet
- Spring wheat and soybeans
- Spring wheat
- Inner Mongolian pasture
- Oasis farming
- Xizang pasture

0 300 600 900 Kilometers
0 100 200 300 400 500 Miles

FIGURE 9-13

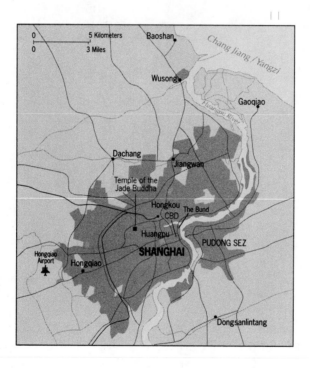

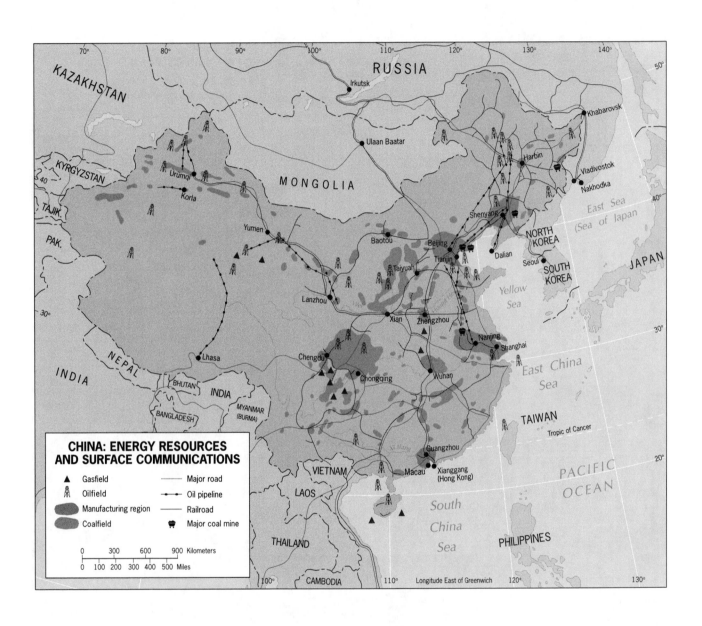

CHINA: ENERGY RESOURCES AND SURFACE COMMUNICATIONS

▲ Gasfield   —— Major road

⚒ Oilfield   •—•— Oil pipeline

Manufacturing region   —— Railroad

Coalfield   ⚒ Major coal mine

0   300   600   900 Kilometers

0   100   200   300   400   500 Miles

FIGURE 9-14

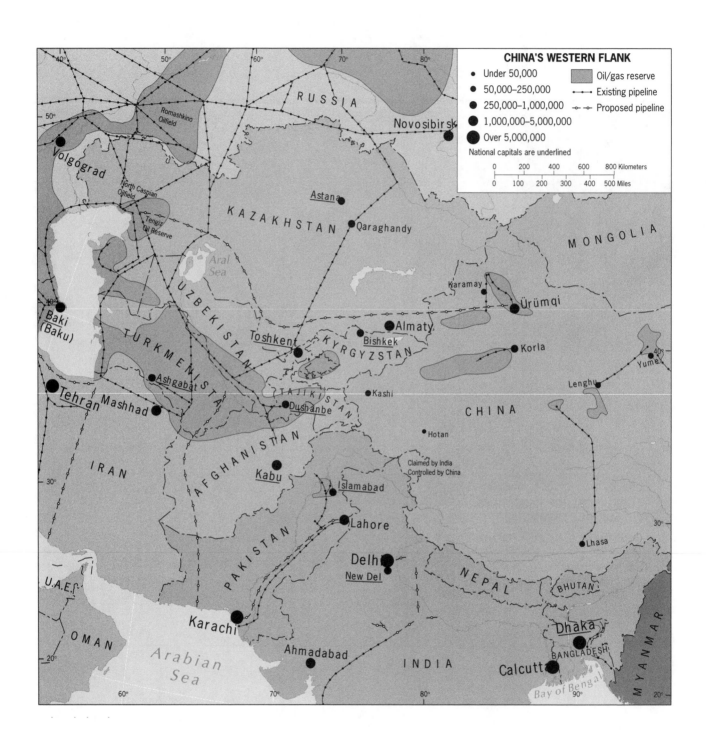

CHINA'S WESTERN FLANK

- Under 50,000
- 50,000–250,000
- 250,000–1,000,000
- 1,000,000–5,000,000
- Over 5,000,000

National capitals are underlined

Oil/gas reserve
Existing pipeline
Proposed pipeline

0   200   400   600   800 Kilometers
0   100   200   300   400   500 Miles

RUSSIA

Novosibirsk

Romashkino Oilfield

Volgograd

North Caspian Oilfield

Tengiz Oil Reserve

Astana

KAZAKHSTAN

Qaraghandy

Aral Sea

MONGOLIA

Karamay

Ürümqi

Baki (Baku)

UZBEKISTAN

Toshkent

TURKMENISTAN

Almaty

Bishkek

Korla

Yume

Lenghu

KYRGYZSTAN

Kashi

CHINA

Ashgabat

TAJIKISTAN

Dushanbe

Tehran   Mashhad

IRAN

AFGHANISTAN

Hotan

Claimed by India
Controlled by China

Kabu

Islamabad

Lhasa

Lahore

Delhi

New Del

NEPAL

BHUTAN

PAKISTAN

U.A.E.

Karachi

OMAN

Arabian Sea

Ahmadabad

INDIA

Dhaka

BANGLADESH

Calcutt

MYANMAR

Bay of Bengal

FIGURE 9-15

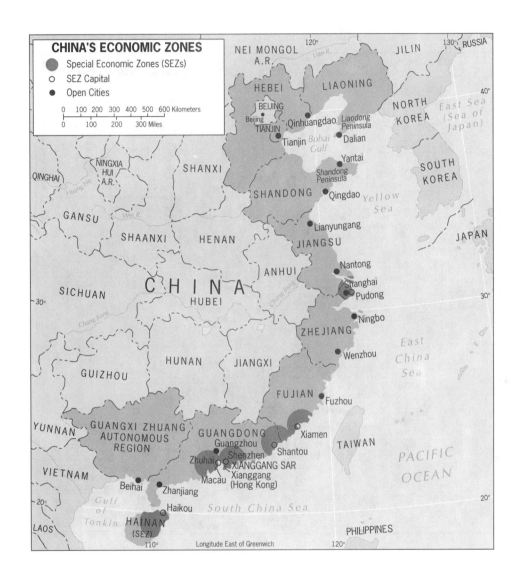

CHINA'S ECONOMIC ZONES

- Special Economic Zones (SEZs)
- ○ SEZ Capital
- ● Open Cities

0 100 200 300 400 500 600 Kilometers
0 100 200 300 Miles

FIGURE 9-16

FIGURE 9-17

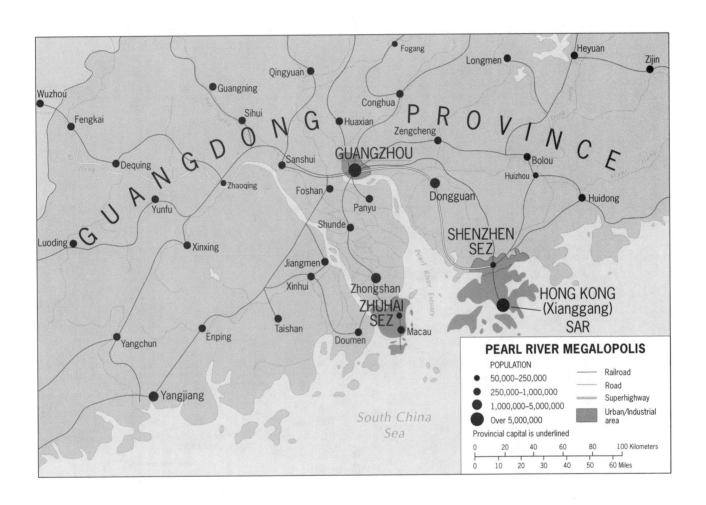

Figure 9-18

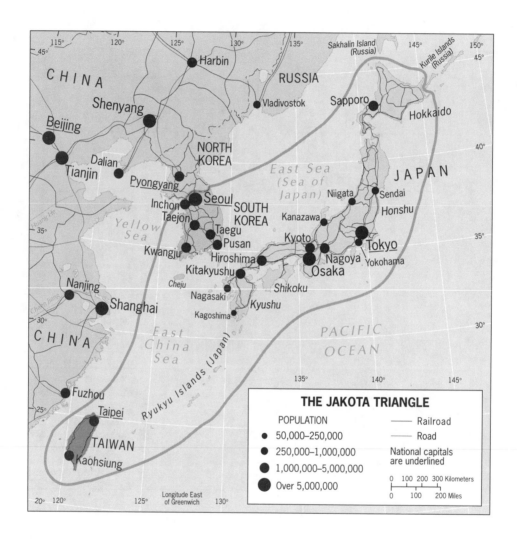

THE JAKOTA TRIANGLE

POPULATION

- • 50,000–250,000
- • 250,000–1,000,000
- ● 1,000,000–5,000,000
- ⬤ Over 5,000,000

—— Railroad
—— Road

National capitals
are underlined

0   100 200 300 Kilometers
0   100   200 Miles

188   **FIGURE 9-19**

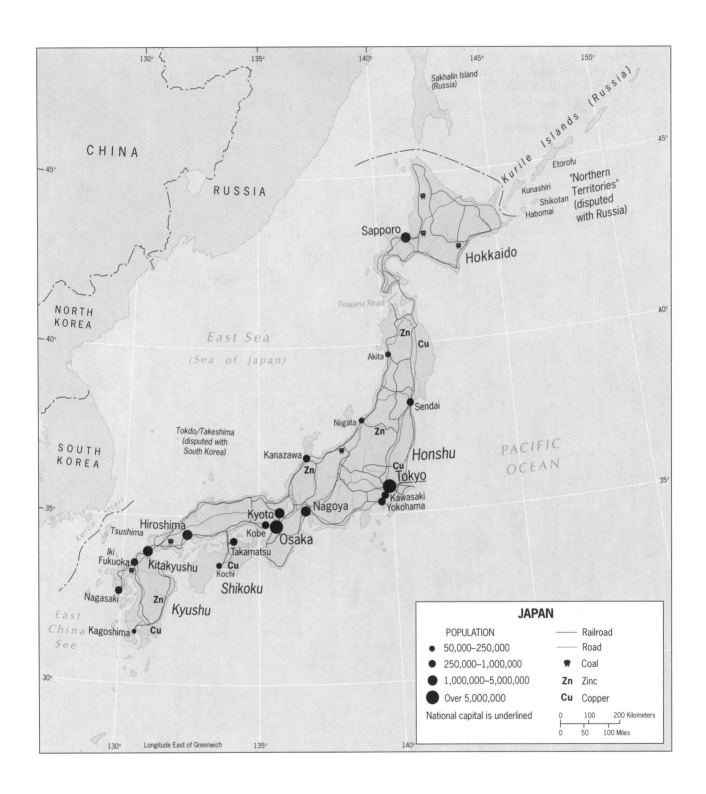

FIGURE 9-20

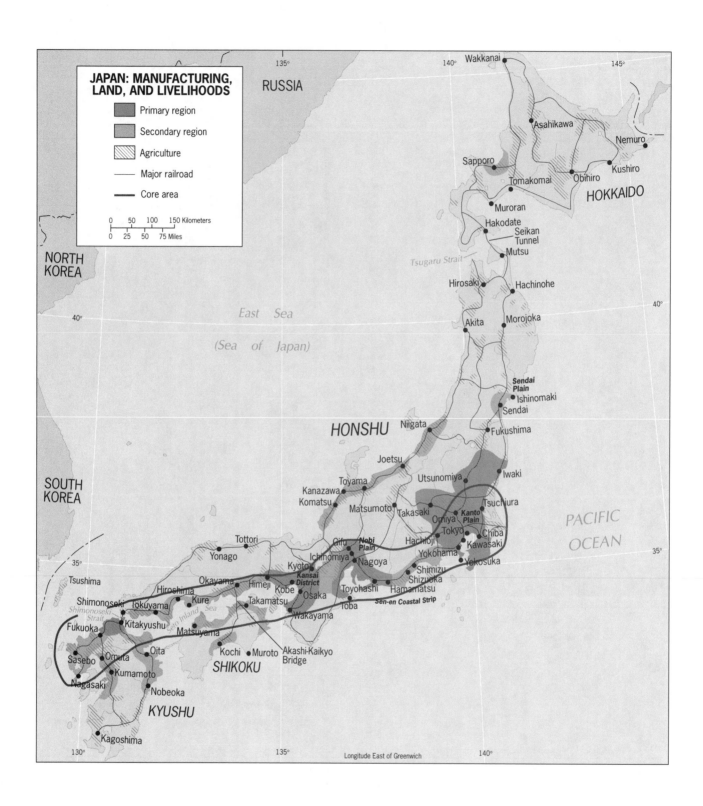

JAPAN: MANUFACTURING, LAND, AND LIVELIHOODS

Primary region
Secondary region
Agriculture
Major railroad
Core area

0   50   100   150 Kilometers
0   25   50   75 Miles

RUSSIA

NORTH KOREA

SOUTH KOREA

East Sea

(Sea of Japan)

HONSHU

PACIFIC OCEAN

Wakkanai
Asahikawa
Nemuro
Sapporo
Tomakomai
Kushiro
Obihiro
HOKKAIDO
Muroran
Hakodate
Seikan Tunnel
Mutsu
Tsugaru Strait
Hirosaki
Hachinohe
Akita
Morojoka
Sendai Plain
Ishinomaki
Sendai
Niigata
Fukushima
Joetsu
Iwaki
Toyama
Utsunomiya
Kanazawa
Komatsu
Tsuchiura
Matsumoto
Takasaki
Kanto Plain
Omiya
Tottori
Gifu
Nobi Plain
Hachioji
Tokyo
Chiba
Yonago
Ichinomiya
Nagoya
Kawasaki
Kyoto
Yokohama
Yokosuka
Kansai District
Shimizu
Okayama
Himeji
Shizuoka
Hiroshima
Kobe
Toyohashi
Hamamatsu
Kure
Takamatsu
Osaka
Shimonoseki
Tokuyama
Toba
Sen-en Coastal Strip
Shimonoseki Strait
Seto Inland Sea
Wakayama
Fukuoka
Kitakyushu
Matsuyama
Sasebo
Oita
Kochi
Muroto
Akashi-Kaikyo Bridge
Omuta
Kumamoto
SHIKOKU
Nagasaki
Nobeoka
KYUSHU
Kagoshima
Tsushima

Longitude East of Greenwich

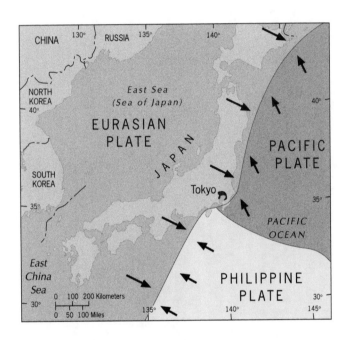

191

FIGURE 9-22

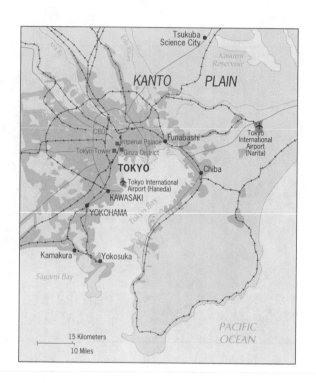

The map shows the Tokyo region with the following labeled features:

Tsukuba Science City

Kasumi Reservoir

Ara R.

Edo River

KANTO PLAIN

CBD

Imperial Palace

Tokyo Tower · Ginza District

Funabashi

Tokyo International Airport (Narita)

TOKYO

Tokyo International Airport (Haneda)

Chiba

KAWASAKI

YOKOHAMA

Tokyo Bay

Kamakura · Yokosuka

Sagami Bay

PACIFIC OCEAN

15 Kilometers
10 Miles

TOKYO

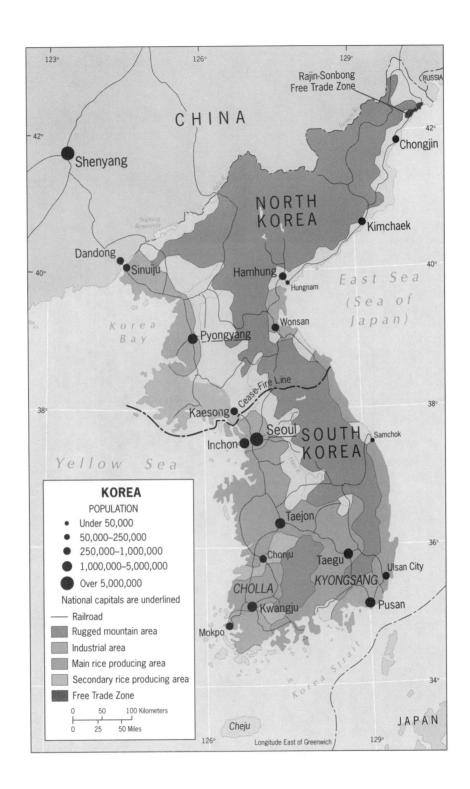

KOREA

POPULATION

- · Under 50,000
- · 50,000–250,000
- ● 250,000–1,000,000
- ● 1,000,000–5,000,000
- ● Over 5,000,000

National capitals are underlined

— Railroad

Rugged mountain area

Industrial area

Main rice producing area

Secondary rice producing area

Free Trade Zone

| 0 | 50 | 100 Kilometers |
| 0 | 25 | 50 Miles |

FIGURE 9-23

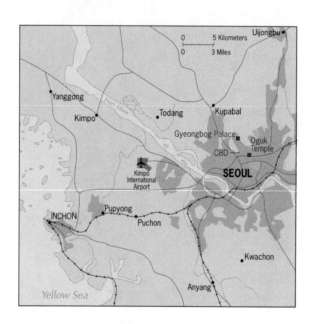

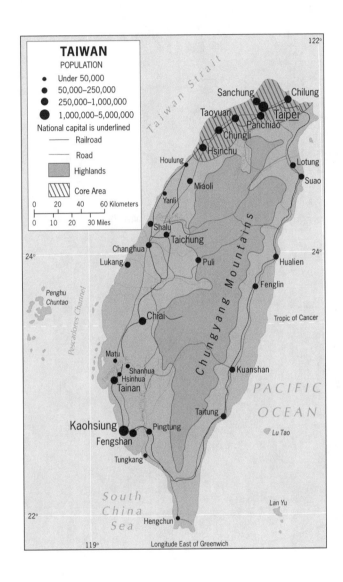

195

FIGURE 9-24

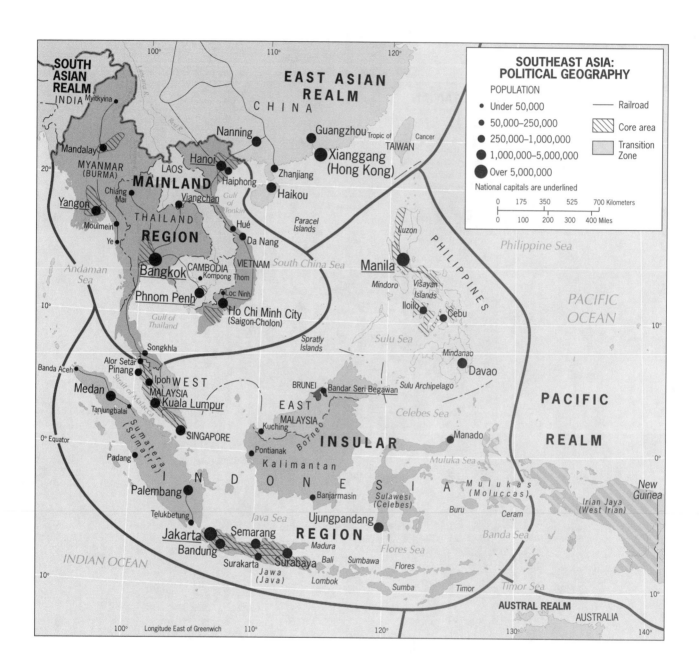

SOUTHEAST ASIA: POLITICAL GEOGRAPHY

POPULATION

- • Under 50,000
- • 50,000–250,000
- ● 250,000–1,000,000
- ● 1,000,000–5,000,000
- ⬤ Over 5,000,000

National capitals are underlined

— Railroad

▨ Core area

▦ Transition Zone

| 0 | 175 | 350 | 525 | 700 Kilometers |
| 0 | 100 | 200 | 300 | 400 Miles |

SOUTH ASIAN REALM

INDIA

EAST ASIAN REALM

CHINA

Myitkyina

Nanning

Guangzhou Tropic of Cancer

TAIWAN

Mandalay

Hanoi

Xianggang (Hong Kong)

MYANMAR (BURMA)

LAOS

Haiphong

Zhanjiang

Haikou

MAINLAND

Chiang Mai

Viangchan

Gulf of Tonkin

Yangon

THAILAND

Hué

Paracel Islands

Philippine Sea

Moulmein

REGION

Da Nang

Luzon

Ye

Bangkok

CAMBODIA

VIETNAM

South China Sea

Manila

PHILIPPINES

PACIFIC OCEAN

Andaman Sea

Kompong Thom

Mindoro

Visayan Islands

Phnom Penh

Loc Ninh

Iloilo

Cebu

Ho Chi Minh City (Saigon-Cholon)

Gulf of Thailand

Spratly Islands

Sulu Sea

Mindanao

Songkhla

Davao

Alor Setar

Pinang

Ipoh WEST

BRUNEI

Bandar Seri Begawan

Sulu Archipelago

PACIFIC

Banda Aceh

MALAYSIA

EAST

Celebes Sea

Medan

Kuala Lumpur

MALAYSIA

Kuching

REALM

Tanjungbalai

Strait of Malacca

SINGAPORE

Borneo

Manado

0° Equator

Sumatera (Sumatra)

Pontianak

INSULAR

Muluka Sea

Padang

Kalimantan

I N D O N E S I A

New Guinea

Palembang

Banjarmasin

Sulawesi (Celebes)

Buru

Ceram

Mulukas (Moluccas)

Irian Jaya (West Irian)

Telukbetung

Java Sea

Ujungpandang

REGION

Flores Sea

Banda Sea

Timor Sea

INDIAN OCEAN

Jakarta

Semarang

Madura

Bandung

Surakarta

Surabaya

Bali

Sumbawa

Flores

Jawa (Java)

Lombok

Sumba

Timor

AUSTRAL REALM

AUSTRALIA

Longitude East of Greenwich

FIGURE 10-2

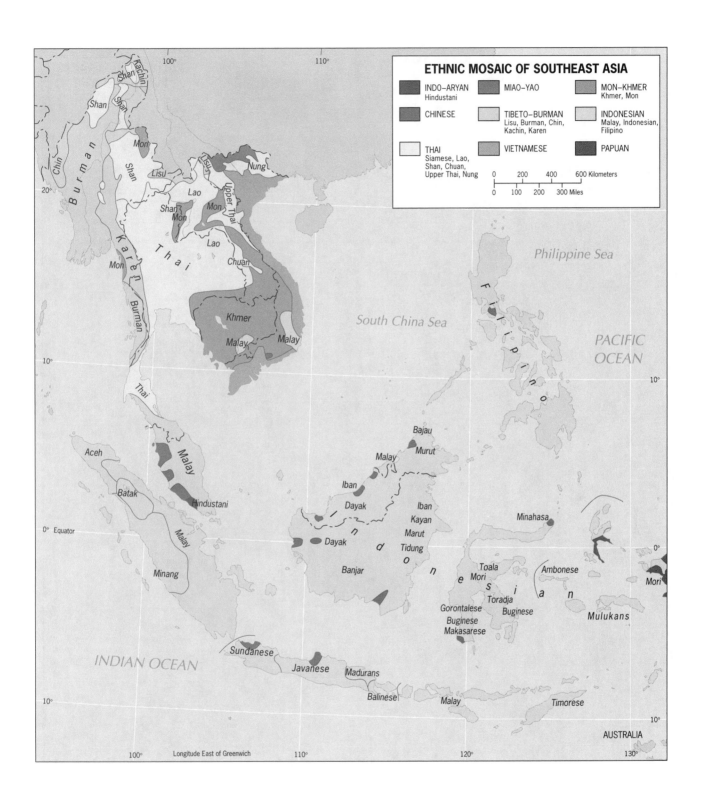

ETHNIC MOSAIC OF SOUTHEAST ASIA

INDO–ARYAN
Hindustani

MIAO–YAO

MON–KHMER
Khmer, Mon

CHINESE

TIBETO–BURMAN
Lisu, Burman, Chin,
Kachin, Karen

INDONESIAN
Malay, Indonesian,
Filipino

THAI
Siamese, Lao,
Shan, Chuan,
Upper Thai, Nung

VIETNAMESE

PAPUAN

0   200   400   600 Kilometers

0   100   200   300 Miles

FIGURE 10-3

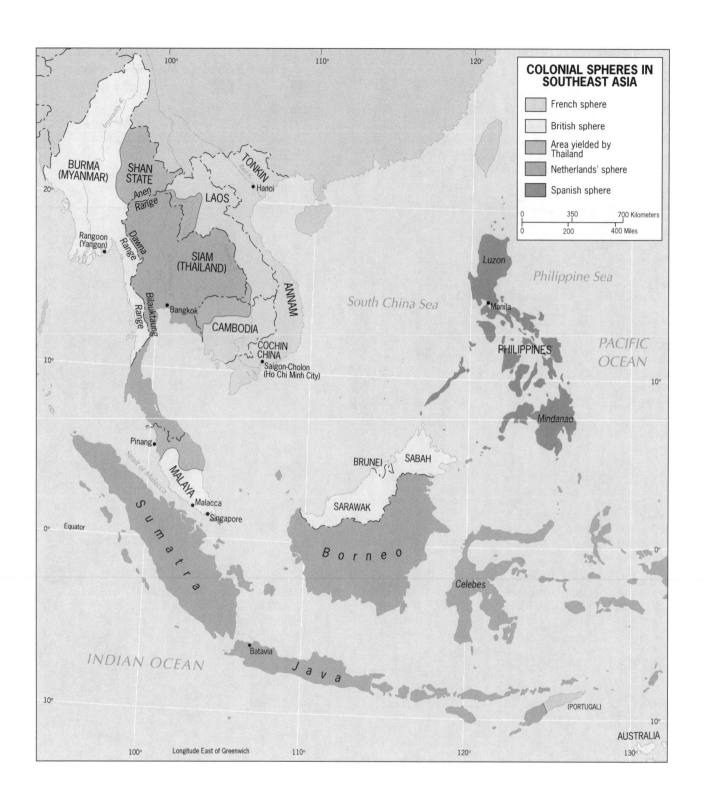

COLONIAL SPHERES IN SOUTHEAST ASIA

- French sphere
- British sphere
- Area yielded by Thailand
- Netherlands' sphere
- Spanish sphere

0   350   700 Kilometers
0   200   400 Miles

BURMA (MYANMAR)

SHAN STATE

Anen Range

Dawna Range

Rangoon (Yangon)

Bilauktaung Range

Irrawaddy R.

TONKIN

Red R.

Hanoi

LAOS

SIAM (THAILAND)

Bangkok

CAMBODIA

ANNAM

COCHIN CHINA

Saigon-Cholon (Ho Chi Minh City)

South China Sea

Luzon

Philippine Sea

Manila

PHILIPPINES

PACIFIC OCEAN

Mindanao

Pinang

Strait of Malacca

MALAYA

Malacca

Singapore

BRUNEI

SABAH

SARAWAK

S u m a t r a

B o r n e o

Celebes

Equator

INDIAN OCEAN

Batavia

J a v a

(PORTUGAL)

AUSTRALIA

Longitude East of Greenwich

FIGURE 10-4

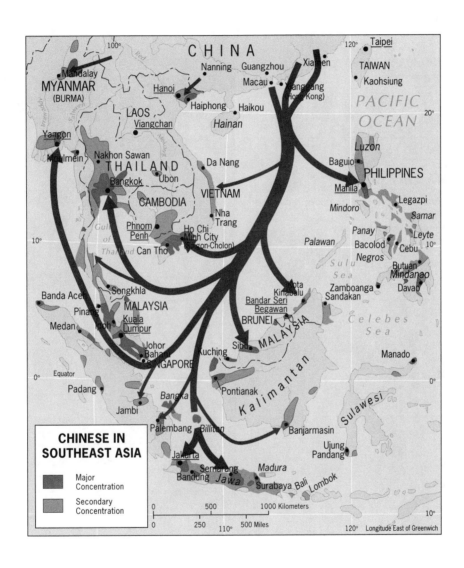

CHINESE IN SOUTHEAST ASIA

- ■ Major Concentration
- ■ Secondary Concentration

FIGURE 10-5

GENETIC POLITICAL BOUNDARY TYPES

ANTECEDENT

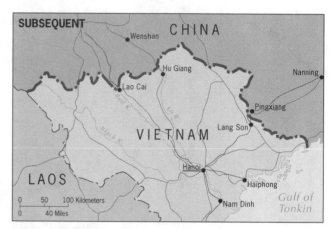

SUBSEQUENT

SUPERIMPOSED

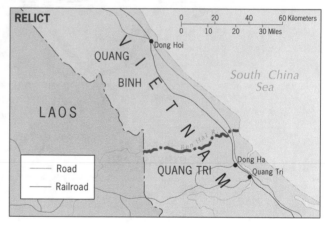

RELICT

FIGURE 10-6

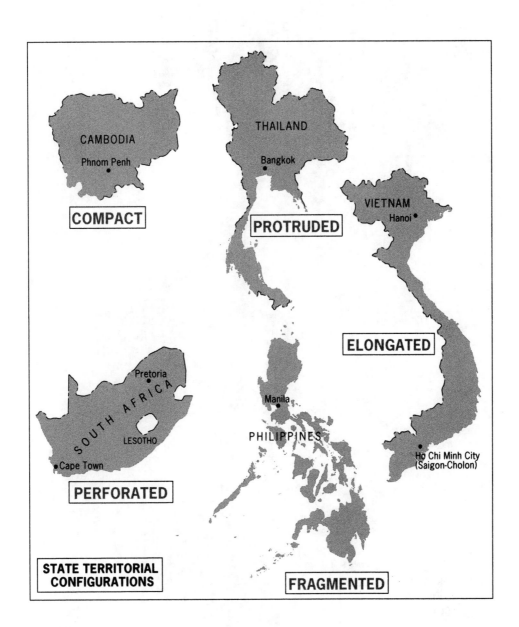

CAMBODIA
Phnom Penh

COMPACT

THAILAND
Bangkok

PROTRUDED

VIETNAM
Hanoi

ELONGATED

Pretoria

SOUTH AFRICA

LESOTHO

Manila

Cape Town

PERFORATED

PHILIPPINES

Ho Chi Minh City
(Saigon-Cholon)

**STATE TERRITORIAL
CONFIGURATIONS**

FRAGMENTED

FIGURE 10-7

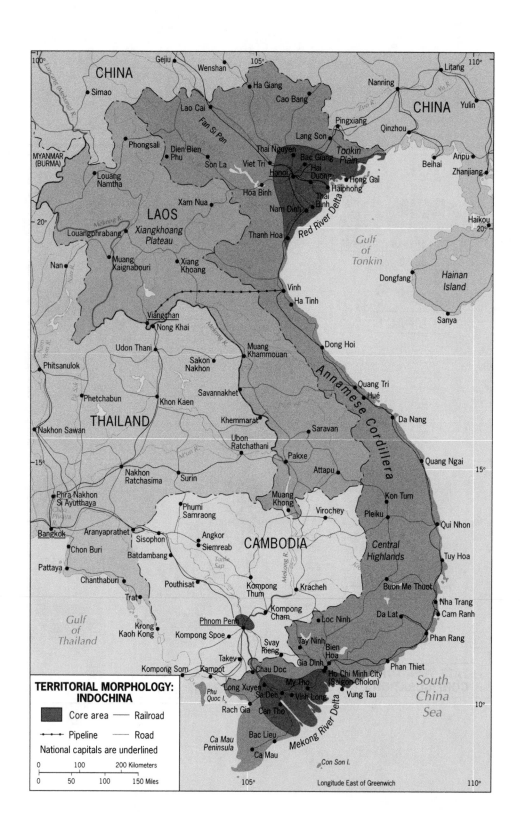

TERRITORIAL MORPHOLOGY: INDOCHINA

- Core area
- Pipeline
- Railroad
- Road

National capitals are underlined

0   100   200 Kilometers
0   50   100   150 Miles

FIGURE 10-8

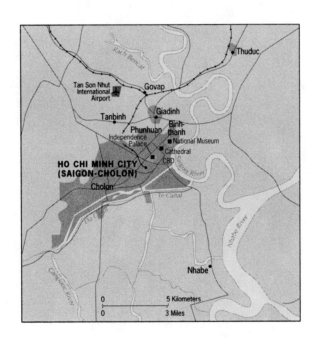

203

SAIGON

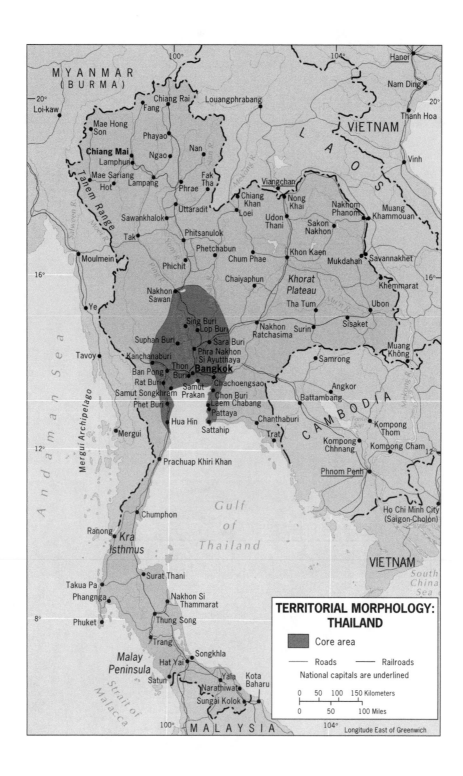

TERRITORIAL MORPHOLOGY: THAILAND

Core area

—— Roads —— Railroads

National capitals are underlined

0   50   100   150 Kilometers

0   50   100 Miles

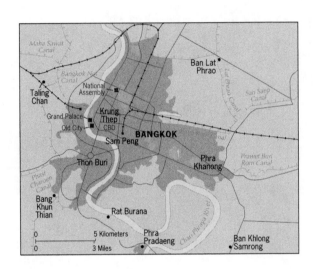

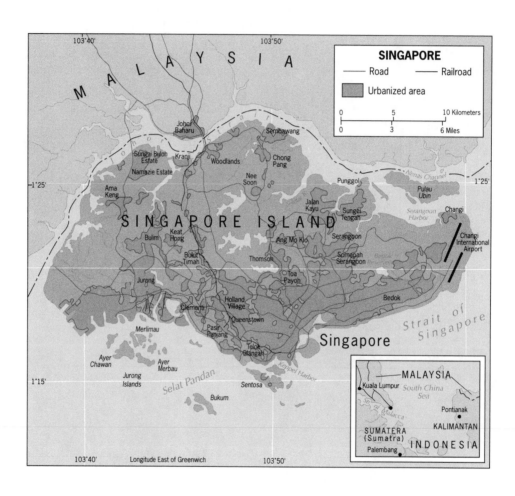

FIGURE 10-10

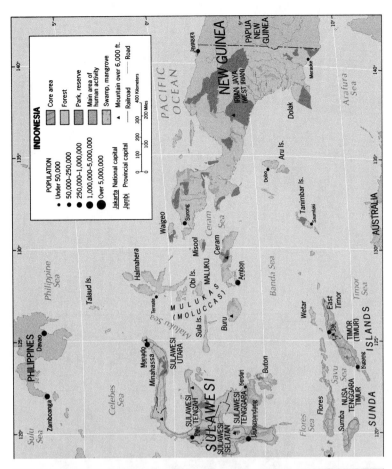

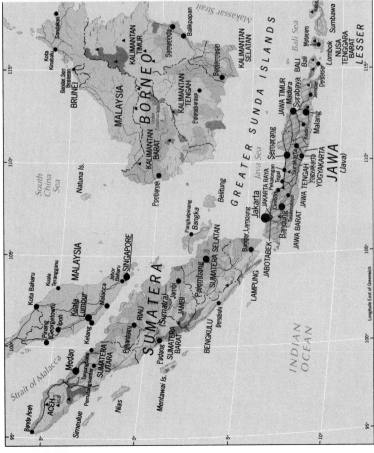

FIGURE 10-11

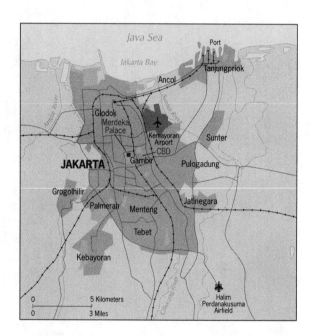

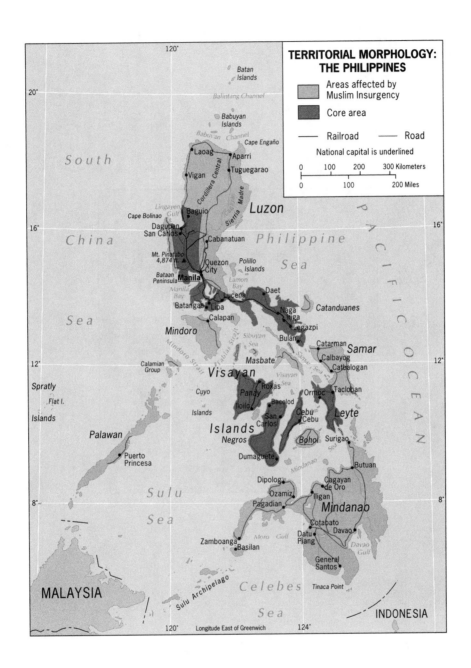

TERRITORIAL MORPHOLOGY: THE PHILIPPINES

Areas affected by Muslim Insurgency

Core area

Railroad   Road

National capital is underlined

0   100   200   300 Kilometers

0   100   200 Miles

FIGURE 10-12

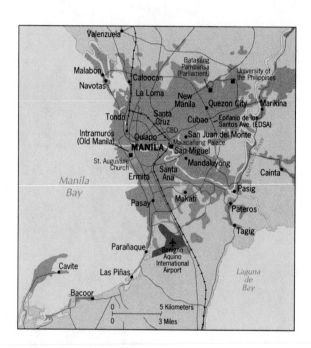

MANILA

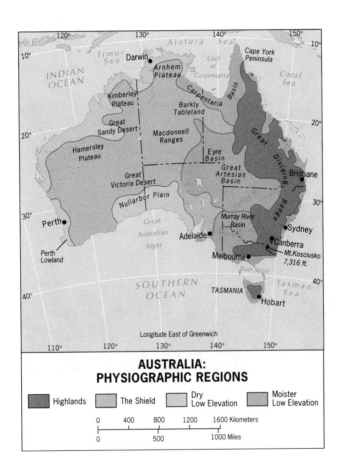

AUSTRALIA: PHYSIOGRAPHIC REGIONS

Highlands | The Shield | Dry Low Elevation | Moister Low Elevation

0 400 800 1200 1600 Kilometers
0 500 1000 Miles

211

FIGURE 11-2

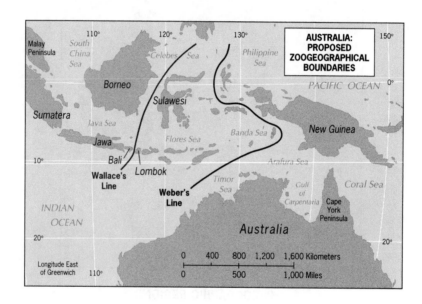

FIGURE 11-3

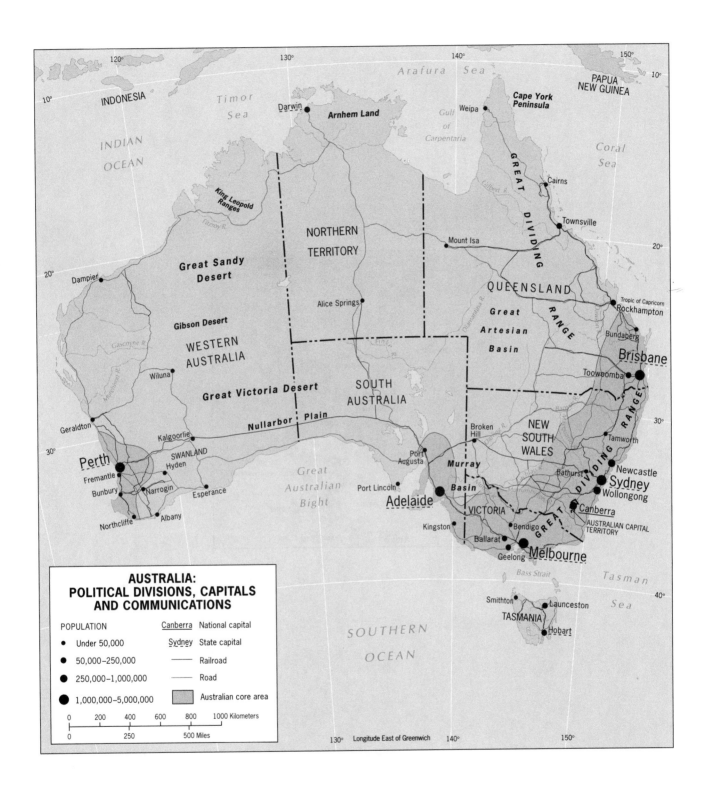

AUSTRALIA: POLITICAL DIVISIONS, CAPITALS AND COMMUNICATIONS

POPULATION

- Under 50,000
- 50,000–250,000
- 250,000–1,000,000
- 1,000,000–5,000,000

Canberra National capital
Sydney State capital
— Railroad
— Road
Australian core area

| 0 | 200 | 400 | 600 | 800 | 1000 Kilometers |

| 0 | 250 | | 500 Miles |

130° Longitude East of Greenwich 140° 150°

213

FIGURE 11-4

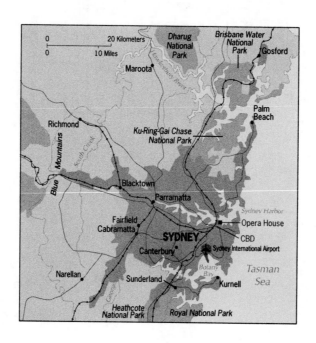

SYDNEY

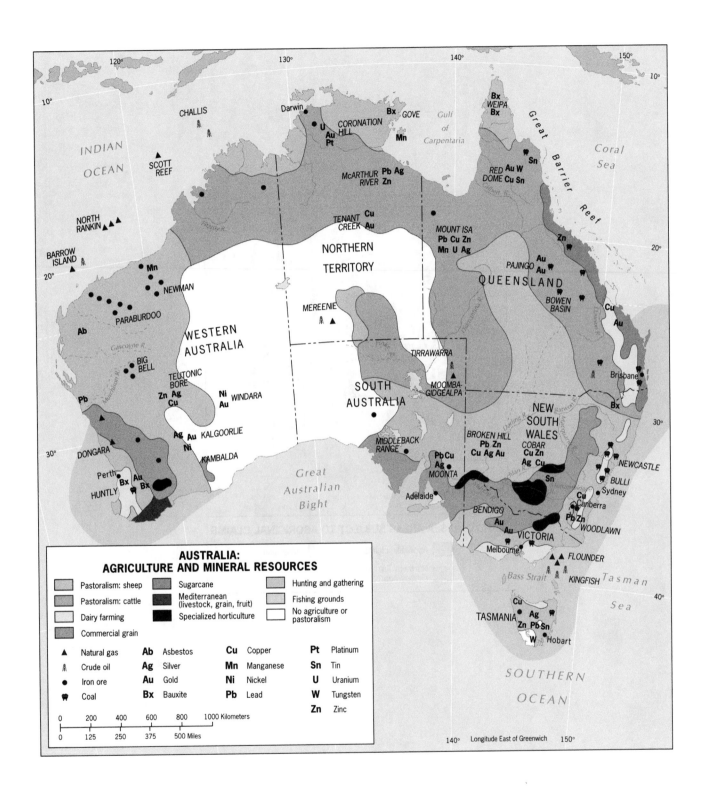

AUSTRALIA:
AGRICULTURE AND MINERAL RESOURCES

Pastoralism: sheep
Pastoralism: cattle
Dairy farming
Commercial grain
Sugarcane
Mediterranean (livestock, grain, fruit)
Specialized horticulture
Hunting and gathering
Fishing grounds
No agriculture or pastoralism

▲ Natural gas
⚒ Crude oil
● Iron ore
🦪 Coal

Ab Asbestos
Ag Silver
Au Gold
Bx Bauxite

Cu Copper
Mn Manganese
Ni Nickel
Pb Lead

Pt Platinum
Sn Tin
U Uranium
W Tungsten
Zn Zinc

0   200   400   600   800   1000 Kilometers
0   125   250   375   500 Miles

140°   Longitude East of Greenwich   150°

215

FIGURE 11-5

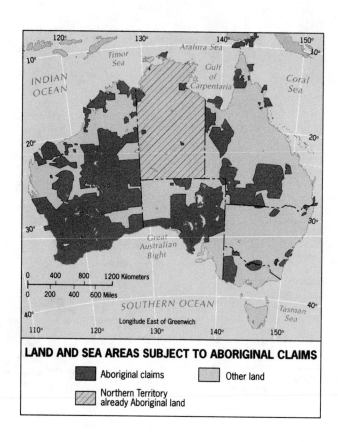

LAND AND SEA AREAS SUBJECT TO ABORIGINAL CLAIMS

■ Aboriginal claims   ☐ Other land

▨ Northern Territory
already Aboriginal land

FIGURE 11-6

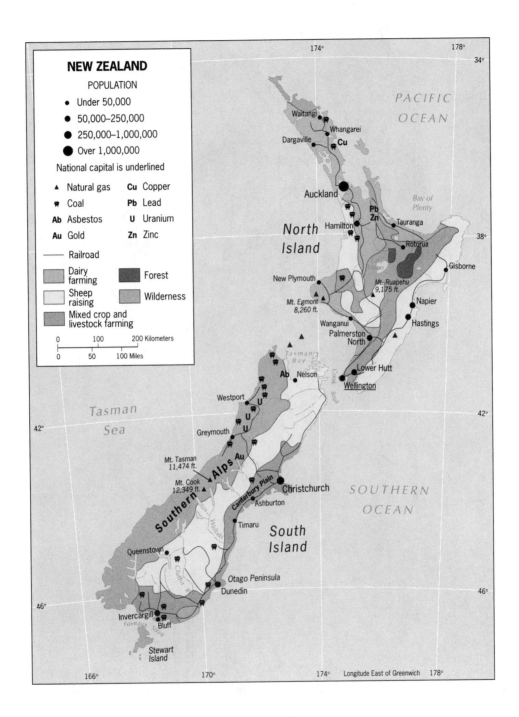

NEW ZEALAND

POPULATION
- Under 50,000
- 50,000–250,000
- 250,000–1,000,000
- Over 1,000,000

National capital is underlined

▲ Natural gas   **Cu** Copper
🏭 Coal   **Pb** Lead
Ab Asbestos   **U** Uranium
Au Gold   **Zn** Zinc

── Railroad

Dairy farming
Sheep raising
Mixed crop and livestock farming
Forest
Wilderness

0   100   200 Kilometers
0   50   100 Miles

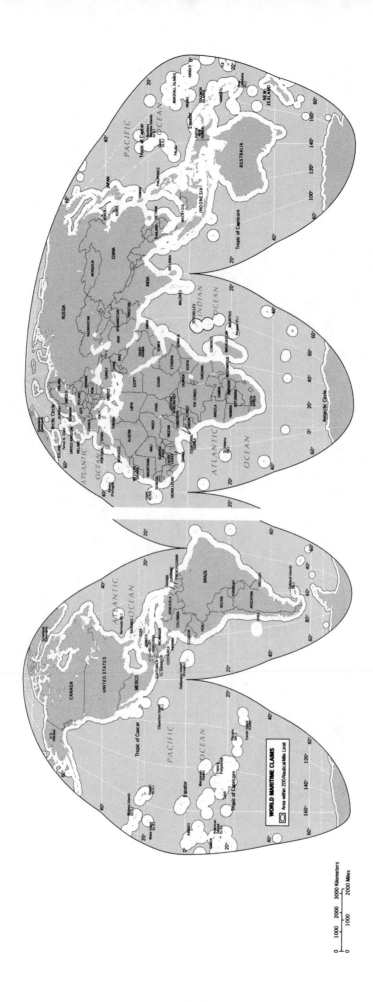

WORLD MARITIME CLAIMS

☐ Area within 200-Nautical-Mile Limit

218

FIGURE 12-2

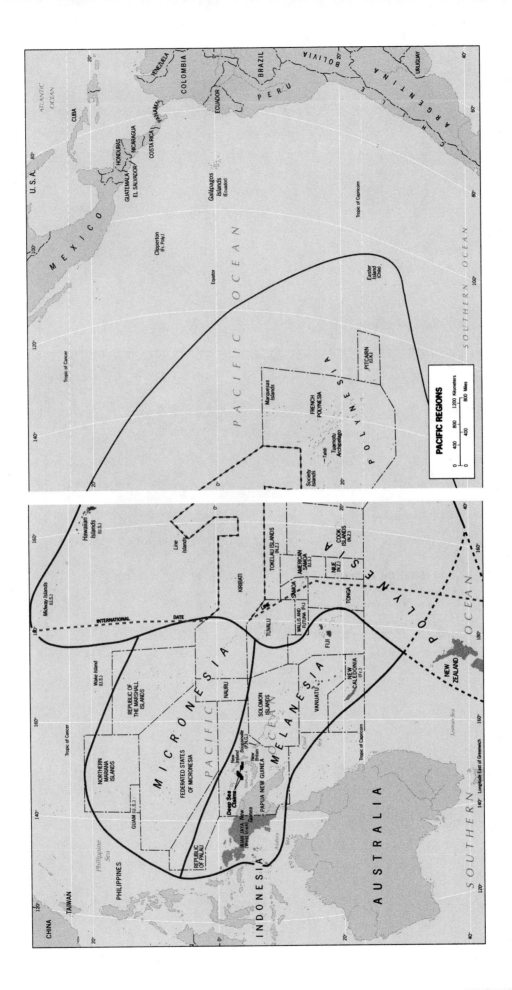

FIGURE 12-3

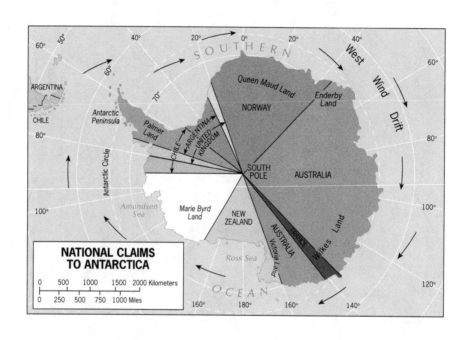

NATIONAL CLAIMS TO ANTARCTICA

FIGURE 12-4

✍ Take Note!

✍ Take Note!

✍ Take Note!

✍ Take Note!

✍ Take Note!

✍ Take Note!

✍ Take Note!

✍ Take Note!

✍ Take Note!

✎ Take Note!

✎ Take Note!